Sing Yer Heart Out for the Lads

Published by Methuen 2002

1 3 5 7 9 10 8 6 4 2

Published in 2002 by
Methuen Publishing Limited
215 Vauxhall Bridge Road,
London SW1V 1EJ

Methuen Publishing Limited Reg. No. 3543167

A CIP catalogue record is available from the British Library.

ISBN 0 413 77251 9

Typeset by SX Composing DTP, Rayleigh, Essex
Printed and bound in Great Britain by
Cox & Wyman Ltd, Reading, Berkshire

Sing Yer Heart Out for the Lads

by Roy Williams

TRANSFORMATION

29 April–21 September 2002

The Lyttelton *Transformation* project is vital to my idea of the National Theatre because it both celebrates and challenges our identity. What do we want the National to be? We must draw on our heritage, on our recent past, and on the talent of the next generation. I want a thriving new audience, including a body of young people under 30 with a theatre-going habit, a new generation of artistic and administrative talent committed to taking the National forward and a realization of the varied potential within this glorious building.

Trevor Nunn Director of the National Theatre

Transformation is thirteen world premieres, hosted in two new theatre spaces, with special low ticket prices. The National's most traditional auditorium, the Lyttelton, has been transformed by a sweep of seats from circle to stage to create a new intimacy between actor and audience. At the same time the Loft has been created – a fully flexible 100-seat theatre. *Transformation* will introduce new generations of theatre makers and theatre audiences to one of the most exciting theatres in the world.

Mick Gordon Artistic Associate
Joseph Smith Associate Producer

Transformation has received major creative input from the Studio – the National Theatre's laboratory for new work and its engine room for new writing – and celebrates the Studio's continuing investment in theatre makers.

Sing Yer Heart Out for the Lads

by Roy Williams

In order of speaking

Gina	JANE HAZLEGROVE
Jimmy, her father	GAWN GRAINGER
Glen, her son	BILLY SEYMOUR
Mark	KOLADE AGBOKE
Duane	OLADAPO TIJANI
Bad T	MARVYN JOHNSON
Lawrie	JOHN MARQUEZ
Becks	CALLUM DIXON
Lee, Lawrie's brother	ALEX WALKINSHAW
Phil	GARY OLIVER
Alan	PAUL COPLEY
Jason	SID MITCHELL
Barry, Mark's brother	FREDDIE ANNOBIL-DODOO
Sharon	KAY BRIDGEMAN
Director	SIMON USHER
Designer	ANTHONY LAMBLE
Lighting Designer	STEVE BARNETT
Sound Designer	RICH WALSH
Company Voice Work	PATSY RODENBURG & KATE GODFREY

Production Manager	Katrina Gilroy
Stage Manager	Stuart Calder
Deputy Stage Manager	Lotte Buchan
Assistant Stage Manager	Marion Marrs
Assistant to the Lighting Designer	Pete Bull
Costume Supervisor	Frances Gager
Wardrobe Assistant	Natalie Titchner
Casting	Toby Whale

SETTING: Saturday 7 October 2000, the King George Public House, South West London

OPENING: Loft, 2 May 2002

KOLADE AGBOKE
MARK

Kolade Agboke trained at Guildhall. **Theatre** includes *Peer Gynt* and *Romeo and Juliet* (National), *Lags* (Tobacco Factory, Bristol), *Love's Labour's Lost* (English Touring Theatre), *The Merchant of Venice* (Sheffield Crucible), *Food for Thought* (Soho Theatre Co), *An Enchanted Land* (Riverside Studios), and *The Ju Ju Girl* (Traverse). **TV:** *The Bill*, *Maisie Raine* and *The Longest Memory*. **Film:** *It Was An Accident* and *Skin Deep*.

FREDDIE ANNOBIL-DODOO
BARRY

Theatre includes *Yerma* (Chipping Norton/tour), *When Brains Don't Count*, *Shining* (Royal Court), *Booked* (Teata Fahodzi), *Things Fall Apart* (West Yorkshire Playhouse/Royal Court), *Beef No Chicken* (Talawa), *Zumbi* and *Just for Kicks* (Black Theatre Co-op), *The Day The Bronx Died* (Tricycle), *Romeo and Juliet* (Half Moon), *Dream for Liberty* (Oval), *Measure for Measure* (Wickham Hall). **TV** includes *Shadow Play*, *Down to Earth*, *As If*, *Casualty*, *The Bill*, *The Vice*. **Film:** *Westway*, *Greenwich Meantime*, *Jump Boys*, *The Final Passage*, *Three Steps to Heaven*.

KAY BRIDGEMAN
SHARON

Kay Bridgeman trained at the Arden School of Theatre. Her **theatre** credits include *King Lear* and *Mules* (at the Contact Theatre), *Mules* and *The Island's Mine* (Covent Garden) and *Talking in Tongues* (Crucible). **TV:** *Holby City*, *Murder in Mind*, *Cutting It*, *The Bill*, *Bhangra Heads*, *Blouse and Skirt* and *Sex Talk*.

PAUL COPLEY
ALAN

Theatre: *For King and Country* (Mermaid, Olivier Award, 1976), *Rita, Sue and Bob Too* (Royal Court), *King Lear* (with Anthony Quayle's Co.), *The Mortal Ash* (Bush), *The Servant* (Birmingham Rep., TMA Award, 1995), *Prin* and *When We Are Married* (West End), *The Ticket of Leave Man* and *The Mysteries* (National) and most recently *The Contractor*

(Oxford Stage Company). **TV:** Ken Loach's *Days of Hope*, *This Life*, *The Lakes*, *Queer as Folk*, *Clocking Off* and *Hornblower*. **Film:** *A Bridge Too Far* and *Zulu Dawn*.

CALLUM DIXON
BECKS

Theatre: *Rozencrantz and Guildenstern*, *The Wind in the Willows* and *Recruiting Officer* (National), *Mr Kolpert*, *A Real Classy Affair*, *The Day I Stood Still*, *Faith* and *Mojo* (Royal Court), *Drummers* (Out of Joint), *Deadwood* (Watermill), *Accrington Pals* and *Mowgli's Jungle* (Octagon, Bolton), *All I Want is an Ugly Sister* (Lilian Baylis), *Waiting at the Water's Edge* (Bush), *Edward II* and *Two Shakespearean Actors* (RSC) and *Macbeth* (British Actors Company). **TV/film:** *Babyjuice Express*, *Hetty Wainthrope Investigates*, *The Knock*, *The Queen's Nose*. **Radio:** *The Wolfgang Chase*.

GAWN GRAINGER
JIMMY

Gawn Grainger's **theatre** credits include *Mutabilitie*, *The Passion* (also touring) and *The Misanthrope* (also in New York) at the National, *Tales From Hollywood* and *Fool For Love* at the Donmar, *Aristocrats* at Chichester Festival Theatre, *Give Me Your Answer Do* at Hampstead and in New York, *Wishbones* at the Bush, *Taking Sides* at Chichester and West End), *Uncle Vanya* at Theatr Clwyd. Also numerous TV and film credits.

JANE HAZLEGROVE
GINA

Theatre includes *Herons* (Royal Court), *Snake in the Grass* (Old Vic), *Wishbones*, *Boom Bang-A-Bang* and *The Mortal Ash* (Bush), *The Wolves* (Paines Plough) and *Heartbreak House* (Coventry). **TV** series include *Silent Witness*, *Without Motive*, *The Cops*, *Hero to Zero*, *London's Burning*, *Making Out*, *Coronation Street* and guest appearances in *Big Smoke*, *The Grand*, *Jonathan Creek*, *Casualty*, *Band of Gold* and *Heartbeat*. **Film** includes *Shooting Star* and *The Whipping Boy*. Also numerous radio plays.

MARVYN JOHNSON
BAD T

Marvyn Johnson attends the Barbara Speake Theatre School. Credits include *Faster for Rogue Films*, a tribute to the Nicholas Brothers at the Theatre Royal, cabaret for Concert Artists International and various commercials.

JOHN MARQUEZ
LAWRIE

Theatre: *Snowbull* (Hampstead Theatre), *From Morning To Midnight* (ENO Coliseum), *Local* (Royal Court), *Baby Doll* (Birmingham Rep., National, Albery), *Small Craft Warnings* (Pleasance), *The Colonel Bird* (Gate), *Romeo and Juliet* (Greenwich), *The End of the Affair* (Salisbury), *A Midsummer Night's Dream*, *The Seagull* (Orange Tree), *All Manner of Means* (BAC), *South Pacific* (Drill Hall), *I Only Want to Be with You* (White Bear), *Last Days of Don Juan*, *An Evening With Gary Lineker* (Birmingham Rep). **TV:** *EastEnders*, *Black Books*, *Jonathan Creek*, *Soldier, Soldier*, *Killing Me Softly*.

SID MITCHELL
JASON

Sid Mitchell's **theatre** credits include *The Dead Eye Boy* at Hampstead, *Lulu* at the Almeida and Kennedy Theatre, Washington DC, *Lift Off* at the Royal Court, Sam Mendes' *Oliver!* at the Palladium and Matthew Bourne's *Swan Lake* at Sadler's Wells. **Film:** *The Invitation* and *Goodbye Charlie Bright*. **TV:** *Holby City*, *Sunburn*, *Summer in the Suburbs* and *Small Potatoes*.

GARY OLIVER
PHIL

Theatre includes *The Cherry Orchard* (National), *Angels in America* (Library), *Squash and The What* (Old Red Lion), *Comedy of Errors* (RSC tour and Young Vic), *Unidentified Human Remains* (Royal Exchange, Manchester), *Salvation* (The Gate), *The Fire Raisers* and *The Slow Approach of Night* (Arts Threshold), *The Lizzie Play* (Theatr Clwyd and tour),

Romeo and Juliet (Factotum Touring Co.), Lorca Festival and The Inkwell (BAC) and The Importance of Being Earnest (Stephen Joseph). **TV** credits include Kavanagh, Heartbeat, Soldier Soldier, Casualty and The Bill. **Film:** Horizontal Man.

BILLY SEYMOUR
GLEN

Billy Seymour trained at the Harris Drama School, Wembley. His **theatre** credits include Herons at the Royal Court. **TV** credits include Brainfood, Modern Time, The Pig Heart Boy and The Bill. **Film:** A Christmas Carol.

OLADAPO TIJANI
DUANE

Oladapo Tijani trains at the Barbara Speake Theatre School. **TV** credits include the forthcoming Fifteen Storeys High.

ALEX WALKINSHAW
LEE

Theatre credits include Lift Off at the Royal Court, The Judas Kiss at The Playhouse and on Broadway and Death in Venice at Glyndebourne Opera Festival. **TV:** Stan The Man, Urban Gothic, Holby City, The Bill, McCallum, Crime and Punishment, Breed of Heroes, Side by Side, A Question of Guilt, Pigboy, Nelson's Column and Anna Lee.

ROY WILLIAMS
WRITER

Theatre: No Boys Cricket Club (Theatre Royal Stratford East), Starstruck (Tricycle), Lift Off, Clubland (Royal Court), Local Boy (Hampstead Theatre), The Gift (Birmingham Rep), Souls (Theatre Centre), Night & Day (Theatre Venture), Josie's Boys (Red Ladder), **TV:** Offside, Bredrens. **Radio:** Homeboys, Tell Tale. **Awards:** 31st John Whiting Award, Alfred Fagan Award 1997 and 1999 EMMA award for Starstruck; The George Devine Award 2000 for Lift Off; Evening Standard Charles Wintour Award for most Promising Playwright 2001 for Clubland.

SIMON USHER
DIRECTOR

Productions include Timon of Athens, Broken Heart, Lover's Melancholy, Pericles, Looking at You (revived) Again, Pale Performer, The Bells, French Without Tears, Winter's Tale, Trios, Lettice and Lovage (Leicester); The Evil Doers, Pond Life, Not Fade Away, Mortal Ash, All of You Mine, Wishbones, Card Boys (Bush); Hamlet, Browning Version, Heartbreak House, Waiting for Godot, Les Liaisons Dangereuses, Whole Lotta Shakin' (Coventry); Herons (Royal Court); Exquisite Sister, Burning Everest (West Yorkshire Playhouse), Twins (Birmingham); Mr Puntila and His Man Matti (Chichester); Great Balls of Fire (West End).

ANTHONY LAMBLE
DESIGNER

Theatre includes Herons (Royal Court), The Contractor, Comedians, (Oxford Stage Company), A Christmas Carol (Chichester Festival Theatre), A Midsummer Night's Dream, As You Like It (NT/Tour), and In Celebration, The Sea, Aristocrats, Retreat From Moscow and The King of Prussia (Minerva, Chichester). Forthcoming productions include The Roman Actor (RSC Swan) and Mother Theresa is Dead (Royal Court). He has designed for many productions in theatre, dance, opera and film and is a course tutor for the Motley Theatre Design Course.

STEVE BARNETT
LIGHTING DESIGNER

Lighting credits include Sparkleshark (National), Carmen and L'elisir d'Amore (Surrey Opera), Bedroom Farce and Blithe Spirit (Redgrave Theatre), Sympathetic Magic (Finborough), La Venexiana (Etcetera) and Evelyn Glennie's multi-media Shadow touring UK and Europe. He has worked at many regional theatres and at the National since 1994 on productions including King Lear (also touring to Greece and Turkey) Skylight and Frogs (NT Education tour) and as Assistant to the Lighting

Designer on My Fair Lady, Peter Pan, A Winter's Tale, The Waiting Room and Mother Courage.

RICH WALSH
SOUND DESIGNER

Previous sound designs include: The Walls (National), Exposure, Under The Blue Sky, On Raftery's Hill, Sacred Heart, Trust, Choice (Royal Court); 50 Revolutions (Whitehall); The Boy Who Left Home, The Nation's Favourite (UK tours), Yllana's 666 (Riverside Studios); Strike Gently Away From Body, Blavatsky (Young Vic Studio); Body And Soul, Soap Opera, The Baltimore Waltz (Upstairs At The Gatehouse), Small Craft Warnings (Pleasance); The Taming of the Shrew, Macbeth (Japanese tour); Dirk, Red Noses (Oxford Playhouse); The Wizard of Oz, The Winter's Tale (Old Fire Station, Oxford).

PRODUCTION CREDITS

Thanks to Paul, Jo and Craig at the North Star pub in Hounslow for help with research for the setting.

The Loft Theatre was created with the help of the Royal National Theatre Foundation.

Many of the projects in the *Transformation* season were developed in the National Theatre Studio.

The *Transformation* season is supported by a gift from the estate of André Deutsch, and by Edward and Elissa Annunziato.

ON WORD graphics designed by typographer Alan Kitching using original wood letters.

The National's workshops are responsible for, on these productions: Armoury; Costume; Props & furniture; Scenic construction; Scenic painting; Wigs

Texts of all plays in the Loft during the *Transformation* season, and of the plays in *Channels* (France) are available from the NT Bookshop at £2. Other volumes of published work by Roy Williams – *Clubland, The Gift* and *Starstruck/ No-Boys Cricket Club* – are also available from the National's Bookshop in the Main Entrance foyer on the Ground Floor.
T: 020 7452 3456; www.nationaltheatre.org.uk/bookshop

TRANSFORMATION SEASON TEAM
ARTISTIC ASSOCIATE Mick Gordon
ASSOCIATE PRODUCER Joseph Smith
ADMINISTRATOR Sarah Nicholson
LOFT THEATRE DESIGNER Will Bowen
FRONT OF HOUSE DESIGNER Jo Maund
PLANNING PROJECT MANAGER Paul Jozefowski
PRODUCTION CO-ORDINATOR Katrina Gilroy
PRODUCTION MANAGER – LOFT REALISATION Jo Maund
PRODUCTION ASSISTANTS – LOFT REALISATION Alan Bain and Gavin Gibson
MODEL MAKERS Riette Hayes-Davies and Aaron Marsden
GRAPHIC DESIGNERS Stephen Cummiskey and Patrick Eley
PROGRAMME EDITOR Dinah Wood
PRESS Lucinda Morrison, Mary Parker, Gemma Gibb
MARKETING David Hamilton-Peters

Thanks to the following people who were part of the original Lyttelton Development Group: Ushi Bagga, Alice Dunne, Annie Eves-Boland, Jonathan Holloway, Gareth James, Mark Jonathan, Holly Kendrick, Paul Jozefowski, Angus MacKechnie, Tim Redfern, Chris Shutt, Matt Strevens, Jane Suffling, Nicola Wilson, Dinah Wood, Lucy Woollatt

TRANSFORMATION SEASON

IN THE LYTTELTON

A co-production between the National Theatre & Théâtre National de Chaillot

The PowerBook .... 9 May–4 June
from a novel by Jeanette Winterson
devised by Jeanette Winterson, Deborah Warner & Fiona Shaw
Director Deborah Warner

A Prayer for Owen Meany .... 10–29 June
a novel by John Irving
adapted by Simon Bent
Director Mick Gordon

A collaboration between the National Theatre & Trestle Theatre Company

The Adventures of the Stoneheads .... 4–13 July
written & directed by Toby Wilsher

A collaboration between the National Theatre & Mamaloucos Circus

The Birds .... 22 July–3 August
by Aristophanes, in a new version by Sean O'Brien
Director Kathryn Hunter

Play Without Words .... 20 August–14 September
devised & directed by Matthew Bourne

IN THE LOFT

Sing Yer Heart Out for the Lads .... 29 April–15 May
by Roy Williams
Director Simon Usher

Free .... 20 May–8 June
by Simon Bowen
Director Thea Sharrock

Life After Life .... 28 May–8 June
a reportage play by Paul Jepson & Tony Parker
Director Paul Jepson

The Shadow of a Boy .... 13–29 June
by Gary Owen
Director Erica Whyman

The Mentalists .... 4–20 July
by Richard Bean
Director Sean Holmes

Sanctuary .... 25 July–10 August
by Tanika Gupta
Director Hettie Macdonald

The Associate .... 15–31 August
by Simon Bent
Director Paul Miller

Closing Time .... 4–21 September
by Owen McCafferty
Director James Kerr

NATIONAL THEATRE STUDIO &
TRANSFORMATION

All the plays in the LOFT are co-produced with the National Theatre Studio. The Studio is the National's laboratory for research and development, providing a workspace outside the confines of the rehearsal room and stage, where artists can experiment and develop their skills.

As part of its training for artists there is an on-going programme of classes, workshops, seminars, courses and masterclasses. Residencies have also been held in Edinburgh, Vilnius, Belfast and South Africa, enabling artists from a wider community to share and exchange experiences.

Central to the Studio's work is a commitment to new writing. The development and support of writers is demonstrated through play readings, workshops, short-term attachments, bursaries and sessions with senior writers. Work developed there continually reaches audiences throughout the country and overseas, on radio, film and television as well as at the National and other theatres. Most recent work includes the award-winning plays *Further than the Furthest Thing* by Zinnie Harris (Tron Theatre, Glasgow; Traverse, Edinburgh, and NT), *The Waiting Room* by Tanika Gupta (NT) and *Gagarin Way* by Gregory Burke (in association with Traverse, Edinburgh; NT; and at the Arts Theatre), *The Walls* by Colin Teevan (NT), *Accomplices* by Simon Bent, *Mr England* by Richard Bean (in association with Sheffield Theatres) and *The Slight Witch* by Paul Lucas (in association with Birmingham Rep), as well as a season of five new plays from around the world with the Gate Theatre, and *Missing Reel* by Toby Jones at the Traverse during the Edinburgh Festival 2001. *Gagarin Way* and *Further than the Furthest Thing* were part of SPRINGBOARDS – a series of partnerships created by the Royal National Theatre Studio with other theatres, enabling work by emerging writers to reach a wider audience.

Direct Action, a collaboration between The Studio and the Young Vic, is an initiative that provides young directors with an opportunity to work on the main stage of the Young Vic. Two plays were co-produced in the autumn of 2001: Max Frisch's *Andorra*, directed by Gregory Thompson; and David Rudkin's *Afore Night Come*, directed by Rufus Norris, who won the Evening Standard award for Best Newcomer for this production.

For the Royal National Theatre Studio

HEAD OF STUDIO	Sue Higginson
STUDIO MANAGER	Matt Strevens
TECHNICAL MANAGER	Eddie Keogh
INTERNATIONAL PROJECTS MANAGER	Philippe Le Moine
RESIDENT DIRECTOR (LOFT)	Paul Miller

NT

Royal National Theatre
South Bank, London SE1 9PX
Box Office: 020 7452 3000
Information: 020 7452 3400

Registered Charity No: 224223

The chief aims of the National, under the direction of Trevor Nunn, are to present a diverse repertoire, embracing classic, new and neglected plays; to present these plays to the very highest standards; and to give audiences a wide choice.

All kinds of other events and services are on offer – short early-evening Platform performances; work for children and education work; free live entertainment both inside and outdoors at holiday times; exhibitions; live foyer music; backstage tours; bookshops; plenty of places to eat and drink; and easy car-parking. The nearby Studio acts as a resource for research and development for actors, writers and directors.

We send productions on tour, both in this country and abroad, and do all we can, through ticket-pricing, to make the NT accessible to everyone.

The National's home on the South Bank, opened in 1976, contains three separate theatres: the Olivier, the Lyttelton, and the Cottesloe and – during Transformation – a fourth: the Loft. It is open to the public all day, six days a week, fifty-two weeks a year. Stage by Stage – an exhibition on the NT's history, can be seen in the Olivier Gallery.

Sing Yer Heart Out for the Lads

Roy Williams

Methuen

Characters

Jimmy, *white, mid fifties*
Alan, *white, late forties*
Lawrie, *white, mid thirties*
Phil, *white, mid thirties*
Gina, *white, early thirties*
Lee, *white, early thirties*
Mark, *black, early thirties*
Sharon, *black, early thirties*
Becks, *white, late twenties*
Barry, *black, early twenties*
Jason, *white, early twenties*
Duane, *black, early teens*
Glen, *white, early teens*
Bad T, *black, early teens*

Act One

King George Public House, south-west London. This section of the bar area is decorated with flags of St George. Windows, walls tables, etc. A huge TV screen is draped in the corner. **Jimmy** *is assembling rows of stools and chairs in front of the TV screen.* **Gina**, *his daughter, is writing names on stickers with a felt-tip pen and sellotaping them on the stools, one by one.*

Gina There had better not be any trouble.

Jimmy Lee will be here.

Gina Lee?

Jimmy He'll sort 'em out.

Gina Lee is juss as bad as they are.

Jimmy He's a copper.

Gina Yer point being?

Jimmy He's a copper, Gina, nuff said.

Gina Get a few pints down him, you'll see. I should know.

She looks at her dad who has the remote for the telly.

You awright over there, Dad?

Jimmy Can't get this fuckin thing to work.

Gina Well, I don't want to hear that, do I?

Jimmy (*looks at screen*) Fucking static.

Gina Leave it to me. (*Takes the remote.*) Wat you done?

Jimmy Nuttin, I was . . .

Gina Pissin about.

Jimmy Oi!

Gina *presses the button on the remote. The screen becomes all blue.*

Jimmy   Piece of shit.

Gina   You finish with the names, I'll do this.

Jimmy   You put Lawrie at the front?

Gina   Yeah. On second thoughts, stick him near the back. He'll only piss about. (*To TV.*) Come on, come on!

Jimmy   Ain't workin.

Gina   The satellite signal ain't comin through. Dad, do me a favour, check that the cable for the dish is plugged in.

Jimmy   Have already.

Gina   What about the dish outside?

Jimmy   Done that.

Gina   Then what is its fucking problem? Where's the instruction manual?

Jimmy   Behind the bar.

Gina   Well, giss it. (**Jimmy** *hands over the manual.*) If I said it once, I've said it a hundred times.

Jimmy   Oh don't start.

Gina   Becks is nuttin but a thievin little git. You should know better.

Jimmy   It was a steal.

Gina   Here we go. Come on, baby, come on, come on . . . (*A picture comes on.*) Yes!

Jimmy   It'll be typical if they called the match off. It's pissing down. We ain't gonna win.

Gina   That's patriotic.

Jimmy   Kevin Keegan is a fucking muppet. Have you seen his line-up? (*Holds up paper.*) Tosser!

Gina   A bit of faith, Dad.

Jimmy Bollocks. He oughta fuck off back to Fulham, be Al Fayed's bleeding lapdog! Never mind manage the national team. A bit of faith, my arse!

Gina What's wrong?

Jimmy Southgate. Keegan has given him the midfield holding position. The midfield holding position, I have trouble even saying it. Look, Southgate is a defender, bloody good one, no argument, but a good passer of the ball, he ain't! I mean Keegan's got Dennis Wise in the frame, why didn't he pick him? Use him? If that ain't torture for the lad, to be picked for the squad, but only to be left on the touchline, whilst some muppet makes a right bollock of the position he's blinding at. I ask you, where's the sense?

Gina Southgate might surprise everyone.

Jimmy Yeah, he'll be more shittier than I thought.

Gina You won't be watchin the match then. You can clear out the backyard at last.

Jimmy Now, I didn't say I weren't gonna watch it. I'm juss stating my opinion, thass all.

Gina Who's up front?

Jimmy Owen and Cole. Andy fucking Cole. Our last game at Wembley an'all. Fucking Keegan.

Gina Does Andy Gray's face look blue to you?

Jimmy Very.

Gina I can't work out anything on this.

Jimmy Let one of the boys do it. Look at his poxy formation.

Gina Dad!

Jimmy 3–5–2! Poxy, continental shit!

Gina Let me guess, 4–4–2?

Jimmy   Too right, 4–4–2. It's the English way of playing: go with summin the lads are comfortable with, fer crying out loud. 3–5–2!

Gina   Dad, yer boring me, shut up! This screen is giving me a headache.

Jimmy   Leave it. They'll be here soon.

Gina   He had better behave himself.

Jimmy   Who?

Gina   Lawrie.

Loud rap music coming from upstairs.

I don't believe him. (*Shouts.*) Glen! Turn it down. Glen! I tell you, I have had it with that bloody kid, he don't answer me no more!

Jimmy   I don't suppose that arsehole of a dad of his has bin to see him.

Gina   You taking the piss? Glen, I swear to fucking Christ!

Jimmy   Let me go.

Gina   What do you think I'm going to do?

Jimmy   I've seen the way you two have been at it lately.

Gina   Drag his arse down here.

Jimmy *goes upstairs to get* **Glen**. **Gina** *lights up a cigarette.* **Jimmy** *returns with* **Glen**, *fourteen and with an attitude.*

Glen   Yeah, wat?

Gina   You deaf?

Glen   No.

Gina   Bloody should be, shit you play.

Glen   Ain't shit.

Jimmy   I can't even understand half the things they're saying.

Glen   Ca you ain't wid it guy.

Gina   English, Glen, we speak English in here.

Glen *sucks his teeth.*

Gina   Excuse me, what was that?

Jimmy   Just tell me what you get from it.

Glen   Loads.

Gina   Yeah, like learning to call a woman a bitch.

Jimmy   You want to listen to music, Glen, the Kinks, Pink Floyd, the Who!

Glen   Who?

Jimmy   You taking the mick?

Glen   Old man.

Jimmy   Oi!

Gina   He ain't bin rude, Dad, he ends every sentence on 'man'. And you know why? Because he's been hanging round with them black kids from the estate, when I specifically told him not to.

Glen   I don't remember that.

Gina   Do not take the piss, Glen.

Glen   Dem boys are awright, Mum.

Gina   No they are not.

Jimmy   Yer mum's right, son, I've seen them, they'll get you in bother.

Gina   They have already. I had to go down his school again, him and his black mates were picking on sum little Asian kid.

Jimmy   What, him? You sure?

Gina   One more strike and he's out.

Glen   I weren't picking on him.

Gina   Not what the teacher said.

Jimmy *clips him on the head.*

Glen   Oi! Move, man!

Jimmy   Little kid thinks he's a hard man now eh? Picking on sum little Asian kid.

Glen   Mum?

Gina   Mum what?

Glen   Tell him.

Gina   You won't always have yer black mates backing you up, you know; one day, those Asian kids are gonna fight back. Prince Naseem was a little Asian kid once, look at him now.

Jimmy   Come on, take yer grandad on, if you think yer hard enuff.

Glen   Will you move from me please.

Gina   All right, Dad.

Jimmy   I hardly touched him.

Gina   It's enuff.

Jimmy   Little girl.

Gina   No more trouble, you hearing me?

Glen (*sees the fag in the ashtray*)   Was that you? Thought you quit.

Gina   I am addressing my addiction.

Glen   See her, Grandad, she fuckin goes on about me . . .

Gina   Oi, oi, less of the fuckin! If I want to have a smoke, I will have a smoke, so shut yer noise. The best thing you can do with temptation, is give in to it – Oscar Wilde.

Glen   Who dat, yer new boyfriend?

Gina   I don't even want to think about what they are not teaching you at school, I really don't. This whole area is going nowhere.

Glen's *mobile phone rings.*

Glen   Who dis? Awright, man, wass up? You joke! Is it! Nuh, man, wat? Yeah, I'm up fer it dread.

Gina *takes the phone off him.*

Glen   Giss it.

Gina (*to phone*)   Hello, this is Glen's mother speaking –

Glen   Mum, no.

Gina   I am afraid he cannot come to the phone, as he is in an awful lot of trouble, and will not be coming out, for the next twenty-five years, feel free to call back then. (*Hangs up.*)

Glen   Yer chat is dry.

Jimmy   What was that he was saying?

Gina   'Nuh, man!'

Jimmy   'Yeah, I'm up fer it dread!' (*Laughs.*)

Glen   You don't hang up on T like that.

Gina   Who?

Glen   T. Bad T.

Gina   Is that his name?

Glen   His street name.

Gina   Wass yer street name?

Glen   Ain't got one yet.

Gina   Ah! (*Pats his cheek.*)

Glen   I won't get it now, yer shamin me.

Jimmy   Yer little whiner.

Glen   I'm sorry.

Gina   Like you mean it!

Glen   SORRY!

Gina   Good.

She *pops her head round the other bar.*

Dad, go give Kelly a hand.

Jimmy   Ware you going?

Gina   Cellars.

Jimmy   Oi, Glenny boy.

Glen   Glen!

Jimmy   Don't get arsey with me, you little shit. Put these names on these seats. Some of the boys have reserved seats for the game.

Glen   Awright if I have a drink?

Jimmy   Yeah of course it is, don't be silly. (**Glen** *strolls to the bar.*) Get out of it! He only believed me. And don't even think about sneaking one away, cos I'll know.

Glen   Cool.

Jimmy *leaves.* **Glen** *pours himself a shot of whisky.* **Jimmy** *creeps up from behind, clips him round the ear, and takes the glass from him.*

Jimmy   Moby. (*Exits.*)

Glen *does as he is told, and puts down the stickers.* **Mark** (*black, early thirties*) *comes in.*

Glen   Awright, man?

Mark   Yeah.

Glen   Wass up?

Mark   What?

Glen   Nuttin.

Mark   Where's yer mum?

Glen   Cellar. Who are you?

Mark   Mark.

Glen   Mark who?

Mark   Juss Mark.

Glen   Awright man, easy guy!

His phone rings again.

(*Answers.*) Who dis? Awright, man. It was my mum weren't
it. She took it off me, wat was I supposed to do, lick her
down or summin? Yeah, so wass up? Wat now? Yeah, well
why didn't you, awright come in.

Two young black kids come in, **Bad T** *and* **Duane**. *They are the*
same age as **Glen**.

Duane   Yes, Glen!

Glen   Awright, man? T?

Bad T   Ware de booze, boy?

Glen   You mad?

Bad T   Did yu juss call me mad?

Glen   No.

Bad T   Did the boy juss call me mad, Duane?

Duane   Musta done! Cos I heard it.

Bad T   Lesson number one, don't ever call T mad, yeah.

Glen   Awright, I'm sorry.

Bad T   S'right. So pass the booze.

Glen   I can't, man.

Bad T   Did the boy jus say he can't, Duane?

Duane   Musta done, T, cos I heard it.

Bad T   Lesson number two, don't ever say you can't, yeah?

Glen   Yeah.

Bad T   Yeah wat?

Glen   Yeah watever, I'm sorry.

Bad T   Better.

Duane   The boy learnin, T. Awright, Mark?

Bad T   Come on, boy, booze! I want a Jack D and Coke.

Glen   My mum will go mad.

Bad T   Mad bitch. 'bout she chat to me like that on the phone.

Duane (*finds a picture of* **Gina** *behind the bar*)   Rah, is that her?

Glen   Yeah, she won, landlady of the year or summin.

Bad T   How much you have in this till?

Glen   T, don't man.

Bad T   Did the boy juss say don't T, Duane?

Duane (*laughing*)   Musta done, cos I heard it.

Bad T   Lesson number three, never say T don't man, yeah? Yeah? Come on?

Glen   Sorry.

Bad T   Good. I was joking anyway yer fool, chill.

Duane   Check his mum, man.

Bad T   Rah!

Duane   Ennit!

Bad T   This yer mum, boy? Fer trut?

Glen   Yeah.

Bad T   Rah!

Duane   Definitely.

Bad T   Definitely would!

Duane   Definitely!

Bad T   She like it on top, Glen?

Glen   Top of wat?

Duane *roars with laughter.*

Glen   Wat?

Bad T   She turn tricks, Glen? Yer mudda turn tricks? You know wat I mean by tricks don't yer?

Glen   Yeah.

Bad T   So, does yer mudda turn tricks?

Glen   Yeah, you mean like card tricks right?

Duane *and* **T** *carry on howling.*

Glen   Wat you saying about my mum, T?

Bad T   Nuttin, forget it, Glen, yer awright.

Duane (*looks at picture of* **Gina** *again*)   Hmmm, oh yes!

Bad T   Definitely!

Glen   Careful, man.

The boys glare at him.

My mum's in the cellar.

Bad T   Did the boy juss tell us to be careful?

Duane   Musta done, cos I . . .

Bad T   Lesson number four, never . . .

Glen   . . . Yeah, I'm sorry.

Bad T   You gotta learn to relax, bredren.

Duane   Ennit.

Bad T   So wat you say, Mark?

Mark   Nuttin. Yer the one doing all the talkin.

Duane   So wass up, Mark, how come you don't come round no more?

Mark   Ask yer mum.

Bad T   Wass this?

Duane   Went out wid my mum ennit.

Bad T   Yer mum's had nuff men.

Mark   You keeping out of trouble, Tyrone?

Bad T   T! Bad T!

Mark   Listen, I used to watch yer mudda change yer nappy, so don't even bother coming to me wid this Bad T business.

Bad T (*eyes* **Glen** *and* **Duane** *laughing*)   Wat you laughin at?

Duane   Nuttin, T.

Glen   Sorry, T.

Duane   You watchin the game today, T?

Bad T   I ain't watchin no rubbish English match. They lose at everyting.

Someone's phone goes off. All the boys reach for their pockets. But it is **Mark***'s that is ringing.*

Mark   Sorry, boys. (*Answers.*) Hi, Karen, wass up? Nuh, he ain't here yet. I don't know, hold up a minute. (*Walks over to a discreet part of the bar.*) Yeah, go on.

Bad T   Rah, Glen, so thass yer phone?

Glen   Smart ennit?

Duane   Smarter than yours, T.

Bad T   Let me see. (*Examines it.*) It's light, wass the reception like?

Glen   Sharp.

Bad T   You get text yeah?

Glen   It's got everything. I can download e-mail, go on Internet and that. Free voicemail.

Duane   Nice, Glen.

Glen   I know.

Mark (*to phone*)   No, I'm stayin here till he comes. I'll come back wid him. How am I suppose to know that, I juss got here.

Bad T   It's so light.

Mark   Cos yer good wid him.

Bad T   Fits into my pocket nice.

Mark   Karen, please don't start, I beg you. I'll see you later.

Bad T   Don't mess up the lining or nuttin.

Glen   Told yer.

Bad T   Sell it to me.

Glen *laughs*.

Bad T   Sell it.

Glen   Nuh, man.

Bad T   Come on.

Glen   I don't want to sell it.

Bad T   Fifteen.

Glen   No.

Bad T   Twenty.

Duane   For that? It's worth twice that . . .

Bad T   You see me talking to you, Duane?

Glen   I don't want to sell it, T.

Bad T   Wat you gonna do wid a phone like this?

Glen   Ring people and that.

Duane   Give the boy back his phone, man.

Bad T   Yeah, but it's too nice fer a white boy like him to have, best let me have it, someone who appreciates it. Look, the fool ain't even got no numbers in his phone book.

Glen   I only bought it the other day.

Bad T   Glen, has anyone, anyone at all, rang you on the phone, besides me?

Glen   No.

Bad T   Anyone ask fer yer number?

Glen   No.

Bad T   So why you reach for it, when Mark's phone rang then?

Glen   I dunno, I juss thought . . .

Bad T   You thought wat, Glen?

Glen   I dunno, juss thought.

Bad T   I'm surprised yer brain can even do that, you thick cunt!

Duane   T man!

Bad T   So much you sellin it to me, Glen?

Glen   Nuttin.

Bad T   Nuttin, you giving it to me fer nuttin, cheers.

Glen   Hold up.

Bad T   Nice.

Glen   I don't wanna sell it.

Bad T   Twelve quid.

Glen   You said twenty a minute ago.

Bad T   Every time you say no, the price goes down. You got a nice jacket too.

Duane   T?

Bad T   Glen?

Glen   I ain't sellin it.

Bad T   Nine.

Glen   I can't.

Bad T   Eight.

Glen   I saved fer months to get it.

Bad T   Six. Keep whining, Glen. You crying now?

Glen   No.

Bad T   Fucking boy's crying, man.

Glen   I ain't.

Bad T   White boy love to cry, ennit, Duane?

Mark   Give the boy back his phone.

Bad T   Excuse me?

Mark   No, excuse you, give the boy back his phone Tyrone.

Bad T   The name's T, right.

Mark   Fuck wat yer name is, give the boy back his phone.

Bad T   Here. (*Hands it back.*) Tek yer fuckin phone. (*To* **Duane**.) And you defendin him.

Duane   All I said was . . .

Bad T   Ca you love the white, man. You want suck him off, ennit? (*To* **Glen**.) It was a joke, Glen, I was jokin wid you. You shouldn't carry on so, someone might juss come and tief up yer life, never mind yer mobile phone.

Gina *comes back to find* **Bad T** *and* **Duane** *behind her bar.*

Gina   Well, make yerself at home, why don't yer? And you are?

Glen   Duane and T.

Gina   Oh, so yer Bad T?

Bad T   I'm big too. (*He and* **Duane** *laugh.*)

Gina   So wat are Duane, and Big T, doing behind my bar? Come on, move, out!

Bad T   You mind?

Gina   No.

Bad T   Don't touch wat you can't afford.

Gina   Is that right?

Bad T   Ennit.

Gina   I will do more than touch, little boy, if you don't shift, never mind ennit.

Duane *and* **T** *ogle over her again.*

Duane   Oh yeah.

Bad T   Definitely.

Gina   You wish.

Bad T   When you lass have black in you?

Mark   Hey!

Gina   Is that supposed to make me quiver?

Mark   Tek yer friend and go home, Tyrone.

Bad T   You my dad?

Mark   No, but I can call him. Do you want him chasin you round the estate wid his leather belt again?

Bad T (*sees* **Duane** *giggling*)   Wat you laughin at? Come!

Duane   Later, Glen.

Bad T   Yeah go kiss yer wife goodbye!

Glen   Hold up.

Bad T   Well come now, if yer comin.

Gina   Ware do you think yer going?

Glen   Yer shamin me, Mum.

Gina   I'll do more than shame yer, if you step one foot out of that door.

Glen   I won't be late.

Gina   You won't be back at all.

Glen   Later. (*Leaves.*)

Gina   He don't listen to a word I say. Like I ain't here. Fuckin kids.

Mark   That Tyrone come juss like his dad, too much mout.

Gina   So?

Mark   So?

Gina   What about you?

Mark   Nuttin.

Gina   How you doing, gorgeous?

Mark   Awright.

Gina   Thought you didn't drink in here no more.

Mark   I thought I'd slum it.

Gina   Cheeky sod. You on leave?

Mark   No I'm out.

Gina   Wat, for good?

Mark   So that was little Glen?

Gina   Little cunt more like. He wants a slap. How's yer dad, Mark?

Mark   So-so.

Gina   I used to see him all the time down the high street, coming out of the betting shop, he would always call me over, sayin hello and that, askin if I have a boyfriend yet.

Mark   Yer still look good, Gina.

Gina   Yeah, yeah.

Mark   You still love to put yerself down. Didn't you see the way those boys were lookin at yer? Yer fit, gal, deal wid it.

Gina   I know someone who will be very pleased to see you.

Mark   No don't.

Gina   Shut up. (*Calls.*) Dad! In here a minute, I got a surprise.

Mark   Oh, look at the time.

Gina   Sit! Dad!

Jimmy Wat?

Gina In here. Fuckin 'ell.

Jimmy (*approaching*) Wat?

Gina Look.

Jimmy Marky boy! How you doin, you awright, son? You look it.

Mark Cheers, Jimmy.

Jimmy Still playing footie, I hope. Pub team are playing this mornin.

Mark Yeah?

Jimmy I still remember when you played for us, blindin he was, blindin! Everyone still talks about that goal you got against the Stag's Head: he ran with it, one end of the pitch to the other he was, no lie. He pissed on that goal Ryan Giggs got for Man U against Arsenal, pissed on it, well and truly pissed on it!

Gina Yeah, Dad, cheers. Punters!

Jimmy We'll talk sum more in a minute, son, you watchin the game?

Mark Na.

Jimmy Na!

Mark I dunno.

Jimmy Behave yerself.

Mark We'll see.

Jimmy Gina, buy him a drink on me. (*Leaves.*)

Gina Yes, sir!

Mark He ain't changed.

Gina So, Mark?

Mark   Yes, Gina?

Gina   We gonna talk about what happened, or are you juss gonna sit there wid yer gob open?

Mark   Let's not. I'm juss looking for my brother, I heard he drinks in here now.

Gina   I was wondering how long it would be before you came back. You see the door? Well, keep yer eyes on it, our pub team will be back any sec. He plays for them. You know he looks juss like you.

Doors swing open. **Lawrie**, **Lee**, *followed by* **Becks** *come in. They do not look happy.*

Gina   Oh shit. Well, come on, how bad was it.

Lawrie   We stuffed the bastards!

The lads cheer.

Boys (*singing*)   Cheer up Duke of Yorks, oh what can it mean, to a, fat landlord bastard, and a, shit football team. (*Chants.*) King George, King George . . .

Gina   You tellin me you useless bastards won?

Becks   3–fuckin–2!

Gina   Oi, Dad, they only bloody won!

Lee   Set 'em up, Gina.

Lawrie   Oh yes, nuttin more sexier than a landlady pouring a smooth top.

Gina   Don't get out much, do yer, Lawrie?

Lawrie   I'll show yer wat I can get out.

Lee   Oi, behave yerself.

Gina   Like I'll be able to see it.

Becks   Nice one, Gina.

Lawrie   Kiss her arse while yer at it.

Gina   Well come on then, blow by blow.

Lawrie   Played them off the field, Gina, gave 'em a fuckin lesson in football.

Becks   Fat cunts.

Lee   It's funny how those fat cunts were 2–0 up.

Lawrie   Only cos of him, I coulda driven a bus through the amount of space he give 'em. Wants shooting.

Becks   Fuck off, Lawrie.

Lawrie   Oooh! You shoulda seen the looks on their faces at half-time, Gina, every one of them, looking like their case was about to come up. Right, thass it I thought, time for my pep talk. I rounded them all up, like this see. (*Demonstrates using* **Lee** *and* **Becks**.) I goes, listen to me, listen to me! Passion! I wanna see some passion. We gotta help each other out, this is no good, we gotta learn to pass to each other, keep control of the ball! (*Screams.*) Look at me! Ain't we?

Lee/Becks   Yeah!

Lawrie   Who are yer?

Lee/Becks   The George.

Lawrie   Who are yer?

Lee/Becks   The George!

Lawrie   Thank you! Well, that was it then, second half, different story. I was going, keep back, keep back, chase, chase, keep the ball, keep the ball –

Lee   Thought he was gonna lose his voice.

Becks   I prayed he would lose his voice.

Lawrie   When Lee got the ball, I tell yer, I heard music, Gina. I goes to him.

Lee   Screaming down my ear he was.

Lawrie Yer tart! I goes, go on, broth, give it a good spin, he places it right into the back, the goalie didn't know wat day it was. Coulda kissed him.

Lee You did.

Lawrie *kisses him again.*

Gina Who got the other two?

Lawrie The black kid, wasshisface?

Becks Barry. Useful, weren't he, Lawrie?

Lawrie Yeah, he was good, the boy done good.

Becks He did more than good, he won the game for us.

Lee Good penalty taker.

Becks Wicked player.

Lawrie Wicked player? Listen to him, trying to sound like a brother.

Becks I'm juss sayin, he won the game for us.

Lawrie Yeah I know wat he did, he's a wicked player, as you so delicately put it. But it was a team effort. He didn't juss win it by himself.

Becks Might as well have.

Lawrie You married to the cunt or wat? The boy did good, no need to break out into a song about it. Worry about yer own football, never mind droolin over wasshisface.

Becks You callin me queer?

Lawrie You got summin to hide, precious?

Gina Ladies?

Becks So wat about you, taking a swing at their captain.

Lawrie Weren't my fault.

Becks   Nor was the goal.

Lee   Will you two lovebirds shut up.

Lawrie   That ref was a knob.

Becks   Now thass true.

Lawrie   That captain of theirs was committing untold fouls, not once did he get his book out.

Lee   Till you opened yer mouth.

Gina   What did he say?

Lawrie   Only the truth.

Lee   Don't tell her.

Lawrie   I accused him of not wanting to book one of his own.

Lee   Arsehole.

Lawrie   Cheers, broth.

Lee   I meant you.

Lawrie   Don't tell me you weren't thinkin it an'all.

Becks   It's true. I saw them havin a right old chat afterwards.

Lawrie   They love stickin together them lot.

Gina   Let me guess, the ref was black?

Lawrie   As soot. Never seen anything so dark.

Lee   Hold it down.

Lawrie   Awright, Mark? Long time no see. Still giving it large in Paddy Land? He lose his tongue or what?

Gina   Behave.

Lawrie   Only askin.

Gina   You've asked.

Lawrie   You know me, Gina, keep the peace.

Gina   Yeah.

Lee   She knows yer.

Lawrie   Got our seats, Gina?

Gina   Have a look.

Lawrie   Oh wass this, you put us at the back.

Gina   Jason asked first.

Lawrie   Fuck that. (*He swaps seats.*) You don't mind, do yer?

Gina   Any trouble, it's you I'm comin for.

Lawrie (*clicks on the remote, picture is blue*)   Gina, wass this, it's all blue.

Gina   Ask yer thievin mate over there.

Lawrie   Becks! You fuckin . . .

Becks   It was workin all right when I sold it to them.

Lawrie (*throws the remote at him*)   Fix it!

Lee   So how you doing, Mark?

Mark   Lee.

Lee   You on leave?

Mark   I quit.

Lee   You joke?

Mark   I had enuff.

Lee   You!

Mark   Yep.

Lee   How's yer dad?

Mark   Up and down . . . Heard about yours. Sorry, yeah.

Lee   S'right. Look, listen, yeah . . .

Mark   Don't.

Lee   Mark . . .

Mark   Don't.

Lawrie   Lee, over here a sec.

Lee   Wat?

Lawrie   Nuttin.

Lee   So wat you callin me for?

Lawrie   Geezer don't wanna know, mate.

Gina (*to* **Becks**)   Wat you fuckin done now?

Becks   I'm adjusting.

Gina   It's black an'white. Juss give us some colour.

Becks   Awright, don't get out of yer pram over it. You reckon we'll win, Lawrie?

Lawrie   We better, restore some pride after that fuck-up in Belgium. I mean, how fuckin bad was that? The nation that gave the world football. (*Roars.*) Come on, you England!

Becks   Come on, England!

Lee   Come on!

Lawrie   2002, boys, make it happen.

Gina   Becks, Becks, stop!

Becks   Wat?

Gina   Weren't you watchin? You had it, picture, it was perfect, colour and everything, go back.

Becks *presses the remote.*

Gina   It's turned blue again.

Becks   Hold up.

The menu comes up on the screen.

Wass this?

Lawrie   It's the menu. Yer pressin the wrong button, you muppet.

Lee   Hold up, Becks?

Becks   Wat now?

Lee   Don't get arsey, I'm tryin to help you here.

Becks   Wat?

Lee   Go to services, on yer right.

Becks   I know.

Lee   Well, go on then.

Becks   Right.

Lee   Click on that. Now, scroll down to picture settings. Click on that. Contrast. Go up.

Gina   Yer going down, he said up.

Lawrie   Prat.

Lee   Up, up.

Becks   I'm going up.

Lee   Awright, yeah thass it, stop! That'll do.

Lawrie   Finally.

Gina   Thank you, Constable.

Lee   Pleasure to be of service, Madam.

Gina   It's good to have someone here with brains.

Becks   Hey, wass keepin them?

Lawrie   They'll be here. Alan won't miss the kick-off, trust me.

Lee   You invited Alan?

Lawrie   Yeah.

Becks   I saw yer mate Darren, Lawrie, going into one about not getting a ticket for the game. Geezer's off his head. He reckons he's gonna stand outside Wembley, give the Germans some verbal. Take them on like he did in Charleroi.

Lawrie   He shat himself in Charleroi. Ran back to the hotel before it all kicked off. It was me giving them Germans some gyp.

Lee   I didn't hear that, did I?

Lawrie   Of course not, Constable.

Becks   What you do?

Lawrie   Wat do you think? We gave them a right spanking. We were in this caff, watching the game. One–nil up right.

Becks (*chants*)   Shearer!

Lawrie   Right, shut up. There was this couple of Krauts sitting nearby, so juss for a laugh, I goes, I gives the old Nazi salute, going like this I was. Fuckin ages I was at it, till finally I catches one of dem giving me the eyeball, I ask wat his problem was, he goes all menstrual, going on about cos they're Germans, it don't make them Nazis, blah, blah, bloody blah! I goes, awright, mate, calm yerself, you a Jew or wat?

Becks *laughs out loud.*

Lawrie   Next minute, the cunt's comin at me comin at me wid a beer bottle. Tiny little cunt he was an'all. I goes, give us that, behave yerself. I take the bottle right off him, give him a slap, stamped on his fuckin head, shoulda seen it, I lean down to him, I goes, Do I take it that yer not a Jew then?

Lee   I didn't hear that, I am so not here.

Mark   You ain't changed.

Lawrie   Did he juss say summin?

Lee   No.

Lawrie   Oi, Mark, you say summin, mate? Mark? You found yer tongue then? Oi?

Lee   Lawrie.

Lawrie   I heard him say summin.

Lee   No you didn't. Let's play.

Lawrie   Have a day off, will yer? Yer off duty.

Gina   Listen to the policeman, Lawrence.

Lawrie   Awright. Well, put the money in.

The boys head for the table football, **Lee** *puts fifty pence in, a ball comes out. The brothers play against each other.*

Becks   Do you know if Rob got a ticket for the match, Lawrie?

Lawrie   He said he'd try. Bastard!

Lee   It's all in the wrist!

Becks   I thought I juss saw his face in the crowd, one of the cameras whizzed by, I'm sure it was him.

Lawrie   Yeah? Give us a shout when you see him next. Oh wat?

Lee   Skill, mate.

Becks   You want to play doubles?

Lawrie   Fuck off, yer worse than me.

Becks   Come on.

Lawrie   Ask our West Indian friend over there.

Becks (*to* **Mark**)   You fancy a game, Mark?

Lee   Leave him alone, Becks.

Mark   Yeah, come, why not.

Becks   I got a partner.

Lawrie   Wat do you want me to do, sing? So, Marcus?

Mark   Mark.

Lawrie   How confident are yer?

Lee   Wat you doing?

Mark *throws down forty quid.*

Mark   This much? Best out of three?

Lee   Mark, don't.

Mark   You my dad?

Lawrie   Exactly, Mark, pay no attention to the old woman. Becks?

Becks   I'm short.

Mark   Don't worry about it.

Becks   Cheers, mate.

Lawrie   Let's play ball.

Mark   You gonna cover the bet?

Lawrie   Lee?

Lee   Oh bloody hell, Lawrie.

Lawrie   Come on.

Lee   Do I look like a cashpoint?

Lawrie   All I got is ten.

Lee   Yer a pain in the arse.

Lawrie   Come on.

Lee   Every time I see you, you cost me money.

Lawrie   Broth? Brother!

Lee   You juss don't listen. (*Gives him thirty.*) You ain't even listening now.

Lawrie   Wat? Joke. Come here. (*Kisses him on the head.*)

Lee   Get off me. I hate it when you do that.

Lawrie   Love yer! Gina, my love, bank this for us, will yer. Let's play ball! Mark, my boy, would you care to kick off.

Mark   No you can.

Lawrie   No yer awright, go ahead.

Mark   I said I'm awright.

Lawrie   Come on.

Mark   You start.

Lee   Will somebody.

Lawrie   Yer missin the point here, Mark.

Mark   Which is what?

Lawrie   You see, this here is my pub, my home from home as it were. You are a guest, I am the host, extending my hospitality.

Mark   I don't want it.

Lee   Fuck's sake, I'll do it.

Lee *drops the ball, they all play.* **Lee** *scores.*

Lawrie   Yes!

Becks   Shit, sorry.

Mark   Don't worry.

Mark *plays the ball. He plays like a lunatic, he is too fast for* **Lawrie** *and* **Lee** *and scores.*

Mark   Yes!

Lawrie   Right, come on, Lee.

Lee *drops the ball in,* **Mark** *is just as fast, if not faster, he scores again.*

Becks   Yes!

Lawrie   Shit. Come on, Lee.

Lee   Awright!

Lee *drops the ball again.* **Mark** *is playing like a maniac now.* **Becks** *just stops and stands back and watches him.* **Mark** *scores.*

Mark   Oh yes!

Lawrie   Bollocks!

Becks   Does it hurt being that good, Mark?

Mark   Torture. Cheers, Gina. (*Collects the money from her.*)

Lawrie   You knew he was useful.

Lee   I knew you wouldn't listen.

Mark   Another please, Gina.

Gina   So you still here?

Mark   Till I see my brother.

Gina   Jimmy will be pleased.

Lee   Still practising?

Mark   Another time, Lee.

Lee   She dumped me as well, you know.

Mark   I don't care about that.

Lee   Sod yer then.

Mark   Right on.

Door opens. **Phil**, **Jason** *and* **Alan** *enter, loud cheering, singing, except* **Alan**, *who walks in coolly, standing between them.* **Lawrie**, **Becks** *and* **Lee** *join their mates in the singing.*

Boys   We're on our way, we are Kev's twenty-two, hear the roar, of the red, white and blue, this time, more than any other, this time, we're gonna find a way, find a way to get it on, time, to get it on together.

Gina   Shall we keep it down, gents? Hi, Phil.

Phil   Awright, Gina.

Gina   So how's life in Watford?

Phil   Sweet as.

Becks   He'll be following their team next.

Phil   Bollocks.

Becks   Giving Elton John a tug.

Phil   Shut it, Becks.

Boys (*sing*)   Don't sit down, with Elton around, or you might get a penis up yer arse!

Gina   Now, now, boys, not in front of the lady.

Alan   It's all right, Gina, I'll keep them in line. (*To screen.*) Come on, lads, got a lot of living up to do.

Phil   We had 'em in June.

Alan   Romania had us in June.

Boys (*sing*)   Come on England, come on England, come on England, let's have another win.

Alan   Where's yer dad?

Gina (*shouts*)   Dad? Like yer haircut, Phil.

Phil   Yeah?

Gina   Yeah, very David Beckham. Suits yer.

The boys start teasing **Phil** *regarding* **Gina**.

Phil   Behave yerselves.

Becks (*watching the screen*)   Commentary's started.

Jason (*roars*) Come on, lads.

Phil   Come on, you England!

Lawrie and **Lee** *join in the roar.* **Jimmy** *appears to get some crisps.*

Jimmy   Wat?

Gina   Yer little friend's here.

Jimmy   Awright, Alan?

Alan   James. Watchin the game?

Jimmy   Be right wid yer, juss serving.

Alan   Lawrie my boy. Good result today, well played.

Lawrie   You remember my kid brother Lee.

Alan   The policeman, you all right, son?

Lee   Yep.

Alan   Spitting image of yer old man, you are. Still a PC?

Lawrie   Detective constable now, if you don't mind, movin to Sutton.

Lee   Lawrie.

Lawrie   Shut up, I don't know why yer keepin it a secret, I'm proud of yer. I kept tellin him it would work out for him, but he never believes me. The state he was in last year.

Alan   State?

Lawrie   Got stabbed.

Alan   Nasty.

Lawrie   Yeah, some coon. It happened at a rave, weren't it, Lee?

Lee   Will you shut up.

Lawrie   He didn't hear, like I care.

Alan   Easy, son.

Boys (*chant*)   ENGLAND, ENGLAND, ENGLAND . . .

Becks   Come on, Rob, ware are yer?

Jason   Wat is he there?

Becks   He was in the crowd a second ago.

Phil   How did he get in? He's banned from every ground in the country.

Lawrie   You think that'll stop Rob? They tried to stop us going into France for '98, we were there though, despite all the efforts and a huge operation by the boys in blue to keep us away. Ooops, sorry, Lee, you didn't hear that. We were there though, oh we were so there.

Jason   You there when the trouble kicked off?

Lawrie   The second Batty missed that penalty, I knew it was gonna kick off. It was fuckin war on the streets. Argies, Krauts, coppers, didn't fuckin matter. We were England!

Alan   Thinking went right out of the window.

Lawrie   Least we were winnin that one.

Alan   You got arrested and thrown in a French cell, you daft sod. Never fight a battle you can't win.

Jason   Wat was Batty doin taking a penalty anyhow?

Mark   Jase?

Jason   Awright, Mark?

Mark   Where's my brother? He was playin today?

Alan   You're Barry's brother?

Mark   Yes.

Alan   You should be proud of him, that boy is useful.

Mark   He ain't a boy.

Alan Easy.

Mark Where is he?

Jason He walked.

Mark While you all drove?

Alan There wasn't enough room. I had a lot of stuff in the back. I'm a painter and decorator. It was hard getting those two muppets in. We drew straws.

Mark And he got the short one.

Alan Yes, he did. What's his problem?

Mark You can talk to me.

Alan No need to fly off, son.

Mark Where's my brother?

Barry *comes in, dancing and singing (New Order's 'World in Motion'); he makes a right show of it, parading himself in front of the lads who are egging him on.* **Barry** *has the flag of St George painted all over his face.*

Barry (*singing*) You've got to hold or kick, and do it at the right time, you can be slow or fast, but you must get to the line, they'll always hit you and hurt you, defend or attack, there's only one way to beat them, get round the back, catch me if you can, cos I'm the England man, wat yer lookin at, is the master plan, we better move with pace, this is a football song, three lions on my chest, I know we can't go wrong! We're singin for England . . .

Boys EN-GER-LAND! We're singin the song, We're singin for England, EN-GER-LAND, Arrivederci, it's one on one! We're singin for England, EN-GER-LAND . . .

Phil Barry, over here!

Barry *goes over to the boys. One by one they take turns rubbing or kissing his bald head.*

Barry Anyone else?

Alan   Yeah, over here, boy . . . (*Rubs his head.*)

Phil   Good boy.

Jason   Fuckin won it for us.

Barry   Thank you, thank you, thank you – (*Sees* **Mark**.) Awright, broth?

Mark   Can I talk to you?

Barry   Game's gonna start.

Mark   Won't take long.

Jason   Got yer seat here, Baz.

Barry   Cheers, Jase.

The teams line up to hear the national anthems. The German one plays first. The lads boo and jeer.

Boys (*to the tune of 'Go West'*)   Stand up, if you won the war! Stand up, if you won the war, stand up, if you won the war . . .

Gina   Feet off the seats, if you please.

*The English national anthem is played. The boys sing along. Some jump on the table, **Gina** protests. They all cheer at the end. The boys then cheer and applaud as each player is called on the TV screen. They do the same when the German team is read out, only this time they jeer.*

Boys (*chant*)   ENGLAND! ENGLAND! ENGLAND!

Alan   Come on, lads.

Lawrie   Let's fuckin have some!

Alan   Lawrence? About wat we spoke about, yer in.

Lawrie   Cheers.

Lee (*approaching*)   Wat was that?

Lawrie   Nosy.

Game kicks off. Boys cheer and applaud.

Mark   Barry?

Barry   Later, Mark, come on, pull up a chair.

Phil   You tell him, boy.

Mark (*grabs him*)   Come here!

Barry   Hey!

Mark   Excuse us!

Mark *ushers his brother into the Gents where they start to bicker.*

Becks   Wass up there?

Lawrie   Must be a black thing.

Becks   Two black geezers in the Gents, dodgy.

Lee   Shut up, Becks.

Becks   Joke.

Phil   Come on, you England!

The boys join **Phil**'s *roar. Lights up on the Gents.*

Barry   I'm missin the start here.

Mark   Wat was that? Dancin like sum spaz, lettin them rub yer head like a genie's lamp.

Barry   They do it at every match, for luck. It's a laugh.

Mark   Wipe that shit off yer face.

Barry   Don't come down here and start, Mark.

Mark   You think I'm here by choice? I feel ill juss bein here. I can't wait to go home so I can have a wash.

Barry   Go home then.

Mark   All this, 'Leave it out, mate, you know wat I mean, I'm a geezer ain't I' –

Barry   Let me watch the match!

Mark   Karen said you ain't bin home fer weeks, wass that about? Too busy to see yer own dad?

Barry   You come to take me back?

Mark   He's askin for yer.

Barry   I ain't seein him.

Mark   Show sum respect.

Barry   For that mess that lies in bed all day? That ain't my dad, why can't he hurry up and die?

Mark   Fuckin little . . .

Barry   Karen feels the same way, you as well. You love to act high and mighty now yer back; where were you when he was gettin sick?

Mark   Look, let's chat when we get home, yeah?

Barry   I'm watchin the game.

Mark   Ware you get that cut on yer neck?

Barry   Romanian fan. Charleroi.

Mark   You were at Charleroi? Fuck's sake.

Barry   Shoulda seen wat I did to him. (*Demonstrates.*) Glassed him right up.

Mark   Why don't you get a tattoo of the Union Jack while yer at it.

Barry *rolls up his shirt. He has a tattoo of the British Bulldog on his lower back.*

Barry   I didn't even pass out. Almost as good as yours, I reckon.

Mark   Wat are you doin to yerself?

Barry   Nuttin you wouldn't do, once.

Mark   I don't want Dad going thru this shit again.

Barry   Fuck off back to the army.

Mark   I'm outta the army, little man, for good.

Barry   Lose yer bottle again, Mark?

Mark   Yer comin home.

Barry   No.

Mark   I'll follow you all day if I have to.

Barry   Do it.

Mark   Kid . . .

Barry   I ain't a fuckin kid no more! You don't understand!

Mark   I don't understand?

Barry   I'm missin it.

Mark   You think yer a badman now, cos yu've had a couple of rucks, kicked a few heads? You've got no idea, son. When yer all alone with a gang of them, havin to fight 'em off by yourself, getting the shit kicked outta yer for yer trouble, you get back to me. It's bollocks, kid. It's their bollocks.

The boys stamp on the floor as they chant to the theme tune of The Great Escape. **Barry** *leaves the loo to watch the match with his mates. He joins in with the chant. The screen turns blue again. The boys protest.*

Gina   Becks, you stupid . . .

Becks   I'll fix it.

Gina   Keep yer bloody hands off.

Lee   Giss it.

Lawrie   Come on, broth.

Lee   Shut up.

Lee *sorts out the contrast. The colour picture comes back. The boys applaud.*

Phil   Nice.

Becks   Juss needs a bit of TLC now and then.

Gina   I want my money back.

Phil   Come on, England!

Boys (*chant*)   ENGLAND! ENGLAND! ENGLAND! . . .

Beck (*mocks*)   Southgate in the middle though.

Phil   When did Cole score last?

Mark   When did he last get a full game?

Gina (*approaching*)   Come on, boys, bunch up.

The boys get all excited by **Gina** *joining them. Cheers, wolf whistles, etc.*

Gina   All barks, no bites. You stayin then, Mark?

Mark   Yeah. Might as well.

Jason   Lampard should be playing.

Phil   An 'ammer playing, behave yerself.

Jimmy   Shut yer hole, Philip. You juss bring on yer bloody Chelsea at Upton Park next week, you'll bloody know it then.

Mobile phone rings. It's **Becks**'*s.*

Becks (*answers*)   Hello. Awright, Rob!

Jason (*shouts*)   Robbie, yer cunt!

Lawrie   Yer wanker!

Becks   Yer hear that? I said did yer hear that?

Lawrie   Ware is he? (*Shouts.*) Ware are yer, yer cunt!

Becks   He's there!

Jason   Wembley?

Becks   Yes, Jase, fuckin Wembley! (*To phone.*) Wat now?
He goes, there's a camera comin into view, he's gonna wave
at us.

Phil   He's there, fuckin 'ell!

They all cheer and wave.

Becks   We see yer, yer there.

They all see Rob from the screen, the boys scream and cheer louder.
Phil *pulls his trousers down and moons at the screen.*

Becks   Rob, Phil is only showin you his arse.

Gina (*to* **Jimmy**)   No trouble eh?

Jimmy   Philip, no more arse!

The boys roar with laughter as they see Rob mooning back at them.

Lawrie   He's only moonin back at us!

Jason   Yer wanker!

Becks   Ring me at half-time, yer nutter!

Lawrie   I tell yer, if we lose again, it's gonna kick off in
there.

Kelly (*off*)   Jimmy?

Jimmy   Kelly needs some help, Gina.

Gina   You better get back there.

Jimmy (*shouts*)   I'll be there in a sec.

Gina   Dad?

Jimmy   Fuck's sake!

The boys laugh as **Jimmy** *has to leave.*

Yeah, yeah, up yours.

Becks   Germans playing three at the back?

Barry   Looks like it.

Jason   Yes, come on, Owen.

Becks   Fuck!

Lee   Good run though.

Barry   He's a fast one.

Alan   Yeah, but then he lost it.

Jason   Nice one, Adams, make him eat dirt.

Lawrie   He's given away a free kick, yer sap.

Phil   Watch the post, watch the fuckin post!

Jason   Good one, Le Saux.

Becks   Doin summin right for once.

Jason   Leave him.

Becks (*acting camp*)   Oooh! (*Blows* **Jason** *a kiss.*)

Jason   Fuck off.

Gina   Nice control by Cole eh?

Lawrie   Yeah, but he's all mouth, no delivery him.

Mark   Cos no one gives him a chance.

Lawrie   Cos he never fuckin scores.

Mark   Shearer played nine games without scoring for England, nine! Didn't stop Venables pickin him.

Lawrie   Cole ain't Shearer.

Mark   He's never bin given a chance to be Shearer.

Barry   Lawrie's right.

Mark   Wat you know?

Barry   Watch him. He needs three or four chances to score a goal, Shearer only needed one.

Mark   He got forty-one goals in one season when he was with Newcastle, how many's he put in for Man U? War'do you want? Since when is a striker judged on how many chances he gets, leave me alone.

Phil   Southgate, you useless piece of shit.

Jason *takes out horn and blows on it, everyone jumps.*

Becks   Jase!

Phil   'kin 'ell.

Jason   Juss tryin to whip up a bit of excitement.

Gina   I'll whip it up yer arse.

Alan   Nice one, Scholes.

Lawrie   Come on, Scholes.

Barry   Get it up.

They sigh as Scholes loses the ball to German player Ballack. Scholes tugs him, Ballack falls. Free kick.

Becks   Wat!

Phil   Hamman won't score.

Barry   He plays for Liverpool ennit.

Hamman shoots from the free kick. He scores. German fans cheer. The boys are stunned.

Phil   Oh wat!

Jason   Nice one, Baz, yer jinxed it.

Barry   Move.

Jason   He did.

Lee   Wat difference it makes, he still scored.

Lawrie   Fuck off Voller, you German cunt!

Boys (*chant*) YER DIRTY GERMAN BASTARD! YER DIRTY GERMAN BASTARD!

Lawrie   Jase, ring Rob, tell him to give one of them Krauts a slap from me.

Alan   There's no point in taking it out on them.

Lawrie   Oh come on.

Alan   We should have had a red shirt in front of the ball. It weren't a strong kick, Seaman should have got that. A blind man could have got that.

Barry   We were well asleep at the back. Hamman saw a chance, he took it.

Alan   Too right he took it. The boy's right.

Phil   Check Keegan's face.

Becks   Yeah, you better be worried.

Jason   He was never cut out to be manager.

Barry   Ain't wat you said when he got the job, going on about him being the people's choice.

Jason   I never said that –

Barry   Lie!

Gina   Can we not bury them yet please.

England are awarded a free kick. Beckham lines up to take it.

Lee   Oh yes!

Lawrie   Come on, Beckham.

Phil   Get it in the box, please.

Jason   Let's have some more reds in there!

Barry   And leave them well exposed at the back, good call, Jase.

Jason   Piss off, Barry.

Barry   Ooh, handbag.

Jason Scores a couple this mornin, and he thinks he's the dog's bollocks.

Beckham crosses the ball. It's headed back.

Gina Get it back. And Philip?

Philip Yeah?

Gina Stop lookin at my tits.

The boys laugh as they tease **Phil**, *calling him a pervert, etc.*

Phil I weren't.

Jimmy (*approaching*) How goes it?

Becks Phil's bin looking at Gina's tits.

Phil I weren't, Jimmy, I swear to God.

Jimmy You'll be prayin to God for your life, mate, if you step out – (*Sees.*) Oh Jesus. One–nil!

Mark Hamman scored a blinder.

Lawrie You a Kraut-lover now?

Alan Easy, Lawrence.

Lawrie It was a poxy free kick.

Mark Watever.

Lawrie No watever about it, boy.

Mark Shut yer hole.

Lawrie Shut my what, wass he say?

Lee Yer missin the match.

Gina Are we happy over there?

Lawrie Sweet as.

Gina Good.

Germans are on the attack, Bierhof is passed the ball. He is in an excellent position to score.

Becks   Shit.

Jason   Flag's up.

Barry   Offside!

Phil   Come on, England!

Jimmy   They wanna stop playin wid themselves!

Cole has the ball, he makes a run.

Phil   Come on, Cole.

Jason   Yes.

Barry   Free kick.

Jason   Which cunt got him?

Gina   Rehmar. Do you know any other words apart from cunt, Jase?

Beckham lines up for another free kick.

Alan   Come on, Beckham.

Gina   I don't care how he talks, he is gorgeous.

Jason   He'll score.

Barry   Got a crystal ball, Jase?

Beckham shoots, he misses.

You were sayin?

Jason   It was on target.

Barry   Yeah, look on the bright side.

Jason   Wass yer problem?

Barry   I'm havin a laugh.

Jason   Leave it out.

Barry   Or wat?

Gina   Girls!

Lawrie   Come on, Owen!

Alan   Ooh, unlucky, son.

Phil   That fuckin coach of theirs looks like Terry McDermott.

Jimmy   He was a good player that Voller.

Alan   How many goals he got when he was playin, Jimmy?

Jimmy   'bout forty-seven. Class player.

Lawrie   For a Kraut.

Alan   Nothing wrong with admiring the enemy once in a while.

Phil   Come on, boys.

Barry   England!

Jason   They wanna take fucking Cole off.

Mark   Why?

Jason   Ain't pullin his weight.

Mark   He ain't alone.

Jason   I'm juss stating my opinion.

Mark   Funny how he's the only black player on the pitch.

The boys protest at that remark.

Gina   Come off it, Mark.

Mark   All I said, it was funny.

Jason   If thass wat I meant, that's wat I woulda said.

Mark   Why him?

Jason   He's playin shit.

Barry   Yer talkin shit.

Mark   Thank you.

Barry   Both of yer.

Mark   Hey, easy.

Jason   Paranoia.

Mark   I'm done.

Mark *goes to the Gents,* **Lee** *follows.*

Lawrie   Ware you going?

Jason   Wass yer brother's problem? He sayin I'm a racist?

Barry   I don't know wat he's doing.

Jason   Wanker.

Lights on in the Gents.

Lee   You don't even like Andy Cole. You told me once, you can't fart loud enough to describe how much you hate Man U, and anyone who plays for them.

Mark   Is it?

Lee   So wat gives? Did you hear that the Post Office recalled their Man U treble commemorative stamps, people couldn't figure out which side to spit on? Wat do Man U fans use for birth control? Their personalities. A man meets up with his mate and sees that his car is a total write-off, all covered with leaves, grass, branches, dirt and blood. He asks his mate, wat happened to yer car? The friend replies, well, I ran over David Beckham. Bloke goes, that explains the blood, but what about the leaves, the grass, and branches and dirt. The geezer says . . .

Mark   . . . he tried to escape runnin by through the park.

Mark *tries hard not to laugh, but gives in a little.. He then heads out.*

Lee   So wat was that shit wid Jason?

Mark   He's a prick.

Lee   I know he's a prick, he ain't a racist.

Mark   Like you?

Lee   Yeah, gwan, Mark, tell half the story.

Mark   Wass there to tell, yer Lawrie's brother.

Lee   You know I ain't like him.

Mark   Wat you gonna do about Alan King?

Lee   He ain't committed an offence.

Mark   Not yet.

Lee   If he does.

Mark   When.

Lee   I'll have him. So wass this about you quittin the army?

Mark   They didn't like the colour of my eyes.

Lee   Oh come on.

Mark   Don't worry yerself.

Lee   I'm gettin married, next month. Her name's Vicky. She's nice, fit.

Mark   Nice one.

Lee   Come to the wedding. Please.

Lights up in the bar.

Barry   Don't tell me we don't have players who know how to pass, it's like we're scared of the ball or summin.

Lawrie (*aside*)   Them and this 'we'.

Alan   You enjoy supporting our boys then, son?

Barry   They're my boys too.

Lawrie   Armchair supporter.

Barry   I bin to Wembley eight times, I never saw you there.

Alan   Wat was yer first game?

Barry   1990, against Yugoslavia. Mark took me.

Alan   Two–one. Bryan Robson, both goals.

Becks   Put the fuckin ball away! Unreal. They don't get better than that.

Lawrie   Fuck this!

Lee (*approaching*)   Where you going? (*Follows.*)

Lawrie *heads for the pool table. He wipes off the names from the board.*

Lee   You can't do that.

Lawrie (*points at his own face*)   Bothered?

Lee   We still got the second half.

Lawrie   They're gonna walk over us, like everyone else!

Lee   Calm down.

Lawrie   Fuckin taking it! Same old shit like Belgium.

Lee   You give up too easily.

Lawrie   So do they. Why do they always do this to us? I wish I was there, give them Kraut bastards summin to laugh about.

Lee   Enough.

Lawrie   They're got no heart, Lee. We give 'em ours, every single game, and we get fuck all back. If those cunts can't do it on the pitch, we can, we will! We're England!

Lee   Yer a prick.

Lawrie   Yer not playing?

Lee   Fuck off.

Alan (*approaching*)   Set 'em up, Lawrie.

Lee *blocks* **Alan***'s path.*

Alan Help you, son?

Lee Leave him alone.

Alan Spittin image of yer old man.

Lee Are you deaf?

Alan Not at all. You and I should have a drink. (*Goes over to* **Lawrie**.) Tragic ennit?

Lawrie Ninety minutes, Alan, to forget about all the shit out there, and they can't even do that.

Alan Your dad would be spinning.

They play pool. **Mark** *is at the bar with* **Gina** *who is pouring him a pint.*

Gina You calm down? Arsehole. You hate Andy Cole.

Mark I know, I'm sorry. Is Barry behavin himself?

Gina Rowdy as the rest of them, nuttin I can't handle. He's all right.

Mark He's stupid. Loves to get led round all the time. The amount of times Mum and Dad had to go to his school, cos of him.

Gina Like you weren't like that as well.

Mark He should listen to wat I'm sayin then ennit?

Gina You and Lee still ain't talkin. I've had blokes fightin over me before, but this is silly.

Mark I knew you'd dump him.

Gina He's gettin married.

Mark He said.

Gina He's brought her in a few times. Posh bit, really nice. Daddy owns a computer company.

Mark You coulda called me.

Gina   And get back wid you, yer mad! I hated myself.

Mark   Don't.

Gina   You two were like that. I got between yer.

Mark   Writing was on the wall long before. He listens to his brother too much.

Gina   And yours don't listen at all.

Mark *rejoins the boys.* **Glen** *comes into the pub, he has been beaten up. He is not wearing his jacket. He tries to sneak in without being seen.*

Jimmy   Glenny boy, get yer arse over here, make yourself useful, clear up the glasses from the table.

Glen   I ain't doin nuttin.

Jimmy   You'll do as yer told, I ain't soft like yer bleedin mum. (*Clocks his face.*) Watcha you run into?

Glen   Don't worry yerself.

Jimmy   Gina?

Glen   No.

Jimmy   Over here.

Gina   Jesus! You bin fighting again? Wass the matter wid you? And ware's yer jacket? Ware's yer fuckin jacket?

Glen   Gone ennit.

Gina   Gone where?

Glen   Juss gone.

Gina   Well you better find out ware's it gone, and get it back.

Glen *winces when* **Gina** *grabs his arm.*

Jimmy   Oh Christ, she barely touched yer.

Gina   Glen?

Glen He took my jacket and my phone ennit? Cos he liked 'em.

Gina Who?

Glen Tyrone. Bad T.

Gina That fuckin little black kid?

Jimmy You let him take it off yer? You didn't even fight back?

Alan All right there, Jimmy?

Jimmy Should be ashamed of yerself.

Alan Jimmy?

Jimmy Some fuckin little black kid has had a pop at my boy.

Gina Little bastard.

Lawrie Who are they?

Jimmy (*to* **Glen**) Stop cryin.

Glen I ain't.

Jimmy Only got a scratch, stand up straight.

Gina Dad?

Jimmy Teach you how to fight, then you can go back, sort 'em out.

Gina Leave him alone. I'm gonna kill the little cunt.

Mark You mean black cunt? (*To* **Barry**.) You gettin this?

Gina Come on, Mark, they were a couple wrong uns you saw 'em yerself, even if I was thinkin it, can you blame me? Wass the matter wid you, look at his face.

Jimmy A poxy scratch.

Gina I call it as I see it.

Mark You all bloody do.

Gina   Would they have nicked his stuff if he was black?

Lawrie   No.

Lee   Ware you goin?

Lawrie   Find this kid.

Lee   Lawrie!

Alan   I'll go.

Lee   You stay. (*Leaves.*)

Becks   You ever seen a more shittier pass than that?

Phil   Come on!

Barry   England!

Jason *comes back with a round of drinks.*

Becks   Wass goin on, Jase?

Jason   Gina's boy got into a fight wid sum black kid.

Phil   As long as he won.

Jason   Only nicked his phone and jacket.

Phil   Little bastard. Sorry, Baz.

Barry   Wat for? (*Screams.*) Come on, you England!

Mark *sits alongside his brother.*

Barry   You still here?

Mark   Juss watchin the game.

Barry   So wat about Dad?

Mark   Karen's lookin after him.

Barry   You don't want to go back home.

Lawrie *and* **Lee** *come in, they have* **Duane**.

Duane   I was comin to give 'em back, right.

Lawrie   Yeah.

Duane   Move, right!

Lawrie   Mouthy little . . .

Duane   Glen, tell 'em man, it weren't me, it was T, right.

Lawrie (*slaps his head*)   You want another?

Mark   Hey, you don't have to hit him.

Lee (*stands between them*)   Let's juss chill, yeah.

Mark   Let the boy go.

Lee   Mark, I swear, I'll arrest yer.

Mark   Me?

Jimmy   Go on, son, game's still playin.

Mark   Fuck the game!

Lee (*to* **Duane**)   Ware's the phone?

Duane *hands it over.*

Duane   I was gonna give it back, I told T, he loves to go too far sometimes, but he don't listen.

Lee   You scared of him?

Duane   Yeah.

Lee   So how come you got the phone and jacket off him?

Duane   I dunno. I juss did.

Lawrie   Lying.

Lee   On yer way.

Duane   Glen, I'm sorry yeah.

Lawrie   He said out!

Duane   Fuck off!

Lawrie *grabs the boy and slings him out.*

Mark   Fuckin . . .

Lawrie   Come on, come on!

Lee   It's over. (*To* **Lawrie**.) Cool it, Lawrie.

Mark   You big it up now ennit?

Jimmy (*to* **Glen**)   See wat trouble you've caused?
Wouldn't happen if you stick up for yerself.

Gina   Dad, if you don't stop goin on at him, I'm gonna
shove this beer glass into yer face! (*To* **Mark**.) And you, sit
down and watch the game.

Alan (*aside*)   Rivers of blood.

Gina   Go upstairs, Glen, clean yer face. Alan, I appreciate
your trade, it's always nice to see yer, but I've told you
before, I don't want to hear that kind of talk in my pub.
Leave that England for whites bollocks outside.

Phil   Fuck's sake!

Jason   Will somebody please score!

Alan   Come on, Jimmy, you know what I'm talking about.

Gina   It's my name above that door.

Alan   I'm sorry, babe, I didn't mean to upset you.

Gina   Then don't say it.

Alan   It's not just me, darling. I've got nothing against the
blacks myself, but even you have to admit we've got a
problem here. There are too many different races all trying
to fit into the same box, how is that supposed to work? Now
they've got our kids, talking like them. It's no wonder you
feel the same.

Gina   I do not.

Alan   But I just heard you call that kid a black cunt.

Gina   Cos they beat up my son.

Becks   Fuckin chase it!

Alan Not because he's black? Come on, Gina.

Becks Chase it!

Alan It's OK, we are all racists, you know.

Becks Come on!

Alan All white people are racists. I heard this black geezer say it once, dead clever. We are racists. We are white, he says. Our history, our culture, our jobs, people on TV, it's all white, if not predominantly. It's not by coincidence, it's by design. Being white is the norm. It always has been. We are the norm. You should have heard him.

Gina Well, he's wrong.

Alan Is he?

Jimmy You were barely on solids when Enoch said his piece, Gina, they were lining to carve him up.

Gina Good.

Jimmy They booted him out of his party. All he said was the truth.

Gina And you agree, you stupid old git.

Jimmy Look at all the trouble we've got now, it's those fucking black kids from that estate that are causing it all. You know that. I can handle the older blacks, Mark's dad used to drink in here, blindin fella. But these young ones really know how to push it, mouthing off all the time, for no good reason, carryin like the world owes them a favour, bollocks.

The boys watching the match let out a huge sigh.

Jason That was so close.

Phil Nice one, Seaman.

Becks Not bad for an Arsenal man.

Jimmy Then there's the immigrants.

Gina   Oh Dad.

Jimmy   It's in the papers, you can't deny it, they're everywhere.

Gina   Where, Dad? Where? Down the high street, in here? Where? I don't see 'em.

Lawrie   Tucked away in their nice council homes.

Gina   I'm not hearing this, Lee?

Lee   Leave me out of it.

Lawrie   He knows it's true.

Lee   You a mind-reader?

Lawrie   I'm yer brother.

Jimmy   Papers don't lie, love.

Gina   They lie on a regular basis when it comes to the likes of you. Throw in a pair of tits and they've got you hypnotised. Can you not prove their point please.

Alan   Gina, love, I don't read papers, I haven't picked one up in years. I read books, and I'm tellin you, it's amazing what you read. Pages of it, reams of it, history, telling you, making valid points that the blacks, the non-whites, have absolutely nothing in common with the Anglo-Saxon Celtic culture.

Gina   The what?

Alan   If they want to practise their black culture and heritage, then they should be allowed to do it in their own part of their world. By all means.

Gina   So whites are superior to blacks?

Alan   Yes, if you like.

Gina   Bollocks.

Alan   Consider this, the blacks lived side by side with the Egyptians for thousands of years, only about twenty miles of

sand separated them. When the Egyptians came into
contact with them, they hadn't even invented the wheel,
which the Egyptians had thousands of years ago, they
couldn't even copy it.

Gina   Maybe they didn't need it.

Alan   They didn't need the wheel? What has the black
man done in the world?

Gina   Thass it! (*Goes back to watching the game.*)

Alan   I'll tell you. When the British and European powers
colonised Africa, the colonies had a high standard of
civilisation, when the decolonialisation came round, we left
these countries economically sound with good
administrative government. As soon as the whites left, those
blacks are killing each other. Now they've got some of the
poorest countries in the world. That's how capable the
blacks are of running their own countries and looking after
themselves. You look at the rest of the black hemisphere, the
Caribbean, rotten with poverty, half of them, now we gave
them the means to run their countries efficiently, but we're
still pumping aid into these countries to keep them afloat.
They can't run themselves; if they can't even live with each
other, why should we be expected to live with them as well?
We gave them everything they had to carry on, look at us,
we won the war militarily, but we lost it in real terms; see
the Germans, Japanese, the two strongest economies in the
world, because their countries had been so completely
destroyed, that money had to be pumped in to rebuild the
industries that support these countries. They've managed it,
why couldn't the blacks whose countries weren't even
destroyed? Why do we always have to keep giving in to their
begging bowls? Money which we could do with ourselves,
never mind how the poor blacks are suffering around the
world.

Lee *gives* **Alan** *a sarcastic, slow hand-clap.*

Alan   You know, Lee, you remind me of this copper I met once, told me this story. This black geezer is parking his car, music blaring out from his speakers. My mate the copper still has to go over and have a word, asks the geezer to turn the music down, neighbours bin complaining. The geezer says no, carrying on like my mate was putting the chains back on him. Anything like that happen to you, Lee?

Lawrie   All the time, par for the course.

Lee   Why don't you tell him my whole life, you seem to know it better than me. (*Goes back to the game.*)

Lawrie (*follows*)   They got no respect, Lee, you know that.

Lee   Yer gonna lecture them about respect, Lawrie?

Jason   We're gonna be 2–0 down.

Becks   We need a goal.

Mark   Doubt it somehow.

Barry   No ideas, not one creative mind.

Jason   Where's Gazza when you need him.

Mark   Gazza of old.

Sharon, **Duane**'s *mum, comes bursting in.*

Sharon   Which one of you bastards hurt my boy?

Jimmy   Gina?

Sharon   Which one of you touch him?

Gina   You wanna calm down please, love.

Sharon   Move!

Gina   Do it, or leave my pub.

Sharon   Yer lucky I don't bring the police, 'bout you rough up my son!

Gina   Yer son nicked my boy's phone.

Sharon Weren't him.

Gina He told you that?

Sharon I said it weren't him. You didn't even give him a chance to explain, you tek one look, see his face, thass it! Hey, don't walk away from me, yer racist bitch!

Gina Wat did you say?

Sharon Yer deaf?

Alan Yer boy was shoutin the odds.

Sharon You can shut yer mout as well. I bet it was you.

Lee Calm down, love.

Sharon Let go of my arm.

Lee I said calm down.

Sharon You the police?

Lee Yes. Now calm yerself down, before I arrest yer.

Sharon Oi, bitch, I ain't finished wid you. Who did it?

Gina Get her out of my face.

Lee Mark, help us out here.

Mark No.

Sharon Don't look yer nose down on me right!

Gina Get out, you silly cow.

Sharon Come mek me, I'll tear yer fuckin eye out.

Lee Leave it!

Sharon *strikes out at* **Lee**. **Lawrie** *screams out his brother's name.* **Lee** *restrains her by twisting her arm behind her back.* **Sharon** *shrieks in pain.*

Lawrie You awright, son?

Lee Yes!

Lawrie   Are you sure?

Mark   Lee!

Lee   You had yer chance, back off.

Phil   Wass goin on?

Becks (*sees the commotion*)   Jesus! Yer brother, Baz.

Barry   So wat?

Mark   Lee, get off her, man.

Lee   I told you, Mark.

Sharon   Bitch!

Lee   Jimmy, call the police.

Act Two

Same location as Act One.

Jason, **Barry**, **Becks** *are watching the game. It is a few minutes into the second half.* **Phil** *is watching the commotion going on outside the window.*

Barry I'd give Posh Spice a fucking good seeing to I would. Fuck her till she screams. I'd strip off all her clothes, her damp and sticky knickers, I'd lay her down on the floor, frig her pussy with my fingers, rubbing away at her clit, till she had an orgasm. Then I'd give her a fuck, long lingering fuck. And she'll take it cos she's juicy and sexed up. I'll find out if she takes it up the arse. I'll do it. You hear me, Beckham? Thass wat I'm gonna do to yer fucking wife, if you don't score some goals!

Jason Easy, Barry.

Barry He's gettin on my nerves.

Becks Ain't he carryin sum injury?

Phil His left knee, I think.

Becks I bet he's thinkin about Man U. They got a Champions League game soon, he don't want to get injured. Playing for England don't mean nuttin to them any more.

Barry Three lions on the shirt.

Becks You'd rather see Man U lose, and England win?

Barry We ain't watchin Man U, we're watchin England; when England play, Man U don't exist. Bloody money they're on.

Phil More police out there, they're tellin that Sharon to shut it.

Jason Wat still? Just cart her off, the mad bitch.

Phil   She's got sum mouth.

Barry (*chants*)   ENGLAND! ENGLAND!

Phil   Now Mark's gettin stuck in, he's gonna get nicked an all, if he ain't careful.

Barry   Come on!

Phil   Now she's mouthin off at Mark.

Jason   Gina?

Phil   Sharon! Tellin him she don't need his help. Barry, shouldn't you be out there?

Barry   ENGLAND!

Phil   Baz!

Barry   Wat?

Phil   He's your brother, you should be backing him up.

Barry   I'm watchin the game.

Becks   You ain't gonna miss anything.

Barry   So why are you still here then?

Jason   Cos we follow England.

Barry   Wat you tryin to say, Jase?

Jason   Nuttin.

Barry   I'm not white enuff for England?

Jason   Oh behave yerself.

Barry   Is it?

Jason   You lot need to chill out.

Barry   Black people.

Jason   Awright, yeah! Black people. Going off on one all the time. Whenever someone says the slightest thing. All yer doing is pissing people off.

Barry   All I'm doing is watching the match.

Jason   So watch it! 'kin 'ell.

Becks   Awright, boys, come on, let's bring out the peace pipe. Look, Kieron Dyer's on, he might do summin. (*Goes behind the bar.*) Who wants a drink, Phil? Come on, free round.

Phil   Awright quick, top this up.

Barry   Sharon is nuttin but a mouthy cow. She wants to get nicked, thass her problem.

Becks   Yes, Baz, watever, mate, calm yerself.

Barry   I am calm.

Becks   Good.

Barry (*chants*)   ENGLAND!

Jimmy *and* **Glen** *come back in.*

Gina   Crazy bitch.

Jimmy   Awright, love.

Gina   She's a fuckin loon. (*To* **Jason** *and* **Barry**.) Get yer bloody feet off my seats.

Jimmy (*to* **Becks**)   Settling in? Get yer arse out of there. Yer a thievin bastard, Julian, juss like yer old man.

Becks   I was gonna pay.

Jimmy   Too right you'll pay, how much you had, you little . . . ?

Jason   He ain't had much, Jimmy, I swear, come on, whose round, Phil?

Phil   Na.

Jason   Yer as tight-arsed as Becks, you.

Barry   I'll get 'em in.

Jason   You got the lass one.

Barry   I don't mind.

Becks   Yeah, Jase, shut up, same again please, Barry my man.

Phil   And me.

Barry *goes to the bar.*

Gina   Sorry for wat I said. That Sharon juss wound me up. You know me, I ain't got a problem with nobody.

Barry   It's awright.

Gina   Yer brother won't see it that way.

Barry   I ain't my brother.

Gina   OK.

Barry   I ain't losin my rag awright.

Gina   OK.

Barry   Stop sayin OK. I'm juss sayin, I'm tellin yer, I'm not my brother. I want to watch the match, wat Mark does is up to him. I don't want to be like 'em. Go all mad all the time, like we've all got an attitude. I don't.

Lee *comes in followed by* **Lawrie** *and* **Alan**.

Lawrie   You soft cunt. I'm talkin to you.

Becks   Wat?

Lawrie   He only tells his mates to let that Sharon off.

Lee   I didn't see the point in taking it through.

Alan   The point was made when they put the cuffs on her.

Lawrie   She only bit one of them.

Alan   You can't change people like that.

Lee   And you juss had to stand there, stirring it.

Lawrie   Lee, she went for yer, she coulda had a knife.

Lee   You see knives everywhere, Lawrie. Whenever we go out, whenever you see a black person, you think they've got a knife.

Lawrie   Well, pardon me for caring.

Lee   I'm awright.

Lawrie   Ungrateful or wat eh? Don't come crying to me when one of them stabs yer again.

Alan   You want to be a bit more grateful, son.

Lee   Get out of my face.

Alan   Comfortable, is it? The fence you're sitting on? Wake up.

Lawrie   Oh leave him. I don't know wass the matter wid him.

Alan   Don't ever lose your rag like that again.

Lawrie   Eh?

Alan   You were this much from getting arrested as well. It seems par for the course with you. Is it any wonder no one listens to us?

Lawrie   Hold up.

Alan   I couldn't believe my eyes when I saw you lot running amok in Belgium this summer. Fighting in the streets, smashing up bars and caffs. What was that?

Lawrie   It's about been English. All the things you've said.

Alan   That wasn't been English, you were acting like a bunch of savages. You were no better than the coons.

Lawrie   It's how I feel.

Alan   That's no excuse.

Lawrie   There's nuttin that makes me wanna say I'm proud to be English.

Alan   No one wants to speak up for you. It's not fashionable.

Lawrie   Right.

Alan   But they want to speak up for the blacks, queers, Pakis, that's fashionable.

Lawrie   Yes!

Alan   You just want to run out and beat the shit out of someone. I understand.

Lawrie   So wass the problem?

Alan   It scares people off.

Lawrie   It don't scare me.

Alan   You don't speak for the country.

Lawrie   So, what?

Alan   It's smart-arses who are in control of this country, on every level, and we have to be as clever. Keep this country white, away from the blacks. They're just marginalising them. Don't let them marginalise us. Gina's right, get your head out of crap like the *Sun*, get down the library, read a book, read ten books.

Lawrie   I hate books.

Alan   Not any more. I'll give you a list. Because knowledge is power. You want to hide something from the black man, put it in a book.

Lawrie   I'd rather kill 'em.

Alan   Read.

They continue their game of pool. **Lee** *is by the bar with* **Gina**. *The lads are still watching the game.*

Jason   We should be wearing our home kit. The blue and white.

Becks   Why?

Jason   We always seem to play worse in our red. Wat do you think?

Phil   I think yer talkin shit.

Jason   Look.

Phil   We wore red in '66, and won.

Becks   We wore white and blue in the semis in Italy and lost.

Barry   We wore all white against the Argies in '98 and lost.

Phil   And in Euro '96, against the fuckin Germans again!

Barry   No we didn't.

Phil   We did lose.

Barry   I mean, we wore all blue for that, yer muppet.

Phil   Oh right. I musta bin thinkin about the other game.

Jason   I hated that blue kit.

Becks   Everyone hated it.

Barry   Our home kit then was all right, I like that. I don't know why they changed it. I really liked the touch of light blue it had, on the collars and cuff, and that bit on the shorts.

Boys (*agreeing*)   Yeah.

Barry   Nice.

Phil   I thought the last one we had was awright as well, with the blue and the red stripes down the sides. With a touch of white on the blue shorts.

Boys (*agreeing*)   Yeah.

Phil   Very nice.

Gina   I don't care what colour she is. She deserves to be carted off. Mouthin off like that.

Lee   Lawrie didn't help. I'm so sick of this. He won't listen.

Gina   He loves his football.

Lee   From the day he was born. Thirtieth July, 1966.

Gina   And?

Lee   Day England won the World Cup.

Gina   Shut up.

Lee   On my life.

Gina   No way!

Lee   Dad wanted to name him after Geoff Hurst. (**Gina** *laughs.*) Mum wouldn't have it. You know how many times I've heard Dad going on about that match, describing every goal? When England ruled the world again for four glorious years, when Enoch, best prime minister we never had, spoke the truth. Lawrie loved that shit.

Gina   Wait till I tell Dad.

Lee   I can't do it, Gina.

Gina   Do wat?

Lee   The job. He's my brother, he gets on my tits, but I feel like agreeing with him sometimes. Cos thass the bitta Dad rubbing off on me. But that's not the kind of copper I want to be. But then I'm thinkin it's too late. Whenever a black geezer comes up to me now, I'm shakin. I'm angry. All I wanted to do that night, Gina, was calm it all down. All the things they moan about on the telly, all the things police officers don't do, that they hate, what they should be doing, well, I was doing it! All of it! I was treating all those people at that rave like people, not black people, but people! I wanted to understand, I was trying to listen, I wanted to prove that not all coppers are the same.

Gina   Lee?

Lee   Then he stabbed me. That fuckin black bastard stabbed me. I ain't racist, Gina, but it's how I felt, it's how I still feel, is that so wrong? That bloke tried to kill me, and he got away with it.

Gina   I ain't judging yer.

Lee   All I wanted to do was help.

Gina   There's yer problem. Don't help them. Don't try to understand them. Do yer job. Don't lose yerself in anger, Lee.

Phil   Oh come on!

Jason   Fuck's sake

Becks   They're gettin comfortable again, we gotta keep possession, gotta push 'em back, see how they like it in their own half for once.

Jason   Oh yu useless wankers, come on. Please! I'm beggin yer!

The boys get excited as Le Saux makes a run.

Yes, yes!

Phil   Come on, Le Saux!

Becks   Come on, Le Saux!

Jason   Fuckin cross it!

German defender heads it away.

Phil   Shit.

Jason   Wass he head that away for? Let us have one, yer greedy cunts!

Barry *leaves his seat.*

Jason   Ware you goin, Baz? Baz? (*Mimics* **Barry**.) All I'm doing is watchin the watch.

Barry *goes to the pool table.*

Barry   My name was on the board.

Alan   Was it?

Barry   I was supposed to be playing next.

Lawrie   Yeah?

Alan   Lawrie?

Lawrie *steps aside as* **Barry** *picks up a cue.*

Alan   We are all friends here.

Barry *and* **Alan** *play pool together.* **Lawrie** *watches on.*

Alan   So, how is it going?

Barry   Awright.

Alan   That was a splendid couple of goals you got this morning. Did you ever think about turning pro?

Barry   Had a trial for Fulham. Didn't cut it.

Alan   Their loss. Who do you follow?

Barry   Man U.

Alan   Man U?

Barry   Ain't they good enough?

Alan   Comedian.

Lawrie   I'd shit on Man U.

Alan   Yes, that is very nice, Lawrie, but no one is asking you, are they? (*To* **Barry**.) Follow your local team, what is the matter with you? It's about loyalty. Family even. You don't choose your family, they are just there, from the moment you are born. Through thick and thin. They're with you, you're with them. You are born in the town of

your team. They are your family as well, your blood. And
every Saturday, you are watching them play, willing them
on to score, then another, and another. Final whistle goes.
And you all roar and cheer. You can't wait till next
Saturday. Starts all over again. And no matter where you
go, where you move. You take them with you, in your heart.
When was the last time you've been to Old Trafford?

Barry   Does it matter? I follow them.

Alan   But do you feel them?

Barry   Course.

Alan   Where were you born?

Barry   Shepherds Bush.

Alan   Queens Park Rangers.

Barry   They're shit.

Alan   They're yer blood.

Barry   I ain't following them.

Alan   Just as you like.

Barry   So who do you follow?

Alan   Aston Villa. What are you laughing at? My dad
followed Villa. I was born in Birmingham. We all moved to
London when I was ten. But I took them with me, in my
heart.

Barry   You still watch them?

Alan   Whenever I can. I can still remember my first game.
My dad took me when I was nine. 1961 it was. We beat
Sheffield Wednesday 4–1. We played them off the Park.
And it was John Dixon's last game for Villa.

Barry   Who?

Alan   One of the best players we ever had. He stayed with
the club for seventeen years. He could score goals as well as

make them and play all five forward positions as well as his own, left half. He was our captain when we won the cup in '57. What a game. I've still got the programme. Still, Man U, are a blinding side, can't argue with that. Your Andy Cole is doing all right for himself, and the other one, wasshisface.

Barry   Dwight Yorke. Used to be one of yours.

Alan   Yes all right, don't rub it in. Class player he was.

Barry   Still is.

Alan   Always smiling. Should have seen the verbal he got from some of the fans though when he came back to Villa, wearing a Man U shirt. Black this, black that! I have never heard anything like it. What was it that them Liverpool fans used to chant at John Barnes when he first started playing for them? Lawrie?

Lawrie   Better dead, than a nigger in red.

Alan   Right. Must be hard for you as well.

Barry   I never get it.

Alan   Well, then you are lucky. Isn't he lucky, Lawrie?

Lawrie   Yeah, he's lucky.

Alan   It's good to hear that. It gives hope to us all. You are a black person who everyone sees as a person first, not their colour.

Barry   I am a person.

Alan   That is what I said. Never mind the ones who only see you as a black person. Have you ever run into those people, son?

Barry   No.

Alan   The ones who think being white is the norm?

Barry   I said no.

Alan Awright, son. I'm just trying to put myself in your shoes. No need to get jumpy.

Barry I'm not jumpy.

Alan I understand where you are coming from, I really do. You're from this country, you live here, born here, but there are still a few, the minority, that won't accept you.

Barry I am accepted.

Alan Course you are. I mean, you're not like the Asians, are you?

Barry Damn right I ain't.

Alan No. I don't see your lot owning hundreds of shops all lined up next to each other down Southall. Cutting yourselves off from the rest of the country. Not speaking the Queen's English. Your lot ain't like that at all. You're sweet with us now. Two shots. It must get to you though, when you meet the ones who just want to know about the black experience.

Barry That ain't me.

Alan White girls, eyeing you up all the time, because they're curious, about the myth. White guys wanting to be your mates, because they are curious as well. Penis envy, hardly acceptance, is it, Barry?

Barry Wass the matter wid yer?

Alan Right-on liberals, stupid lefties, all lining up, wanting to do you all a favour, they're just scared you'll lose yer tempers, mug them after work, how equal is that? All that talk, understanding, deep down they know, they believe, blacks are inferior, whites are superior. You must feel really small when you meet people like that . . .

Barry . . . Look, juss fuck off, awright!

Barry *rejoins the others.*

Alan Barry? Barry son?

Lawrie   Wat was that?

Alan   Reeling them in, throwing them back. The boy's got no idea who his friends are.

Phil   Oh look, he's bringin a sub on.

Becks   Oh nice one, Keegan, yer muppet!

Barry (*screams*)   Come on, you England!

Jason   Baz?

Barry   Stand up, if you won the war! Stand up, if you won the war!

Jason   Not again.

Barry   You dirty German bastard! You dirty German bastard!

Jason   Barry!

Barry   ENGLAND!

Jimmy   Oi, Lionel Ritchie, keep it down yeah.

Mark *comes back into the pub.*

Jimmy   You going to be nice now?

Mark   Leave me alone, Jimmy.

Jimmy   I can't do that. Leave the attitude outside, Mark.

Mark   I'm juss watching the game.

Jimmy   Wat happened to that happy little smilin coloured kid I used to know eh? Good little boy? Go on, sit down.

Mark *joins the boys, he sits near* **Lee**.

Jason   Wat do you call that?

Lee   You go to the station?

Mark   They had to drag her in there.

Lee   She was resisting arrest, Mark.

Mark   Like an animal.

Lee   Wat were they supposed to do?

Mark   Four coppers, one woman.

Lee   You saw how she was.

Mark   Four coppers, one woman.

Lee   You never listen, it's your point of view or nuttin.

Jimmy   Mark?

Lee   We're all right, Jimmy. (*To* **Mark**.) I tried to calm the situation as well as I could.

Mark   You takin the piss?

Lee *goes to the bar.*

Mark   Wat you runnin for?

Lee   Top it up, Gina.

Mark   Wat you runnin for?

Gina   Leave it out, Mark.

Mark   You really think she deserved to be treated like that?

Lee   Why you always pushin me?

Mark   Do yer, Lee?

Gina   He was doing his job.

Mark   Stick together, like old times ennit?

Gina   Oh piss off!

Lee   Bloody . . .

Mark   Say it, Lee, call me a nigger again.

Lee   He really wants me to.

Mark   It's wat I am!

Gina   Will you stop.

Mark   You didn't want me havin her cos I was black.

Gina   Oh Mark.

Lee   White guy steals white girl from black guy, it juss doesn't happen, does it, Mark? It's the other way round.

Mark   You wanted to finish wid me cos I was black.

Gina   I finished wid you cos you were boring. You were boring in bed, and you were boring to talk to. If you woke up tomorrow as white as I am, you'll still be boring.

Jimmy (*approaching*)   I warned you, son, come on.

Gina   Leave it alone, Dad.

Barry   ENGERLAND! ENGERLAND! ENGERLAND!

Becks   Awright, Baz, Jesus!

Gina   Will you sort him out please.

Mark (*approaching*)   Barry, come on.

Barry   Wass up, bro? My brother! He's more English than any of you, he's protected this country. He's protected you! Come on, you England! Stand up if you won the war!

Gina   Take him home.

Barry   Game ain't finished.

Mark   He'll be awright. Come on!

Becks   Wat again? They tugging each other's plonkers or wat?

Lights on **Barry** *and* **Mark** *in the Gents.*

Barry   Fucking bastard! 'bout I ain't English.

Mark   Who?

Barry   That geezer Alan. Talkin to me like I'm stupid.

Mark   You shoulda stayed away from him.

Barry   Shoulda told him about Euro '96. Wembley,
Holland, the game!

Mark   I know.

Barry   We killed them, oh man, we killed them! Four
goals, class written all over them. The best match since '66.
Saw it wid me own eyes. You, me and Lee. Cheering the
lads on, singing our hearts out. I backed you and Lee up
when those bunch of Dutch fans tried to have a pop, we
kicked every bit of shit out of them. Then we roared, right
into their faces, England! Shoulda told him that, then give
him a fuckin slap.

Mark   See? They only pretend to be yer friends.

Barry   I don't have problems with the rest of them.

Mark   Not yet.

Barry   What are we, a couple of Pakis now? Wass
happened to you?

Mark   I juss saw Sharon dragged by her hair.

Barry   So what, she's a loudmouth bitch. You told me
yerself, thass why you dumped her.

Mark   So, she deserve that?

Barry   Stop using her as an excuse.

Mark   I ain't.

Barry   You are.

Mark   Look, yer right, I don't want to go home either. I
don't want to see Dad like that. So let's get out of here,
check out Daryl and dem, I bet they're watchin the match.

Barry   I don't like Daryl and his mates.

Mark   You shouldn't be afraid of yer own people.

Barry   I ain't afraid of them, I juss don't like some of 'em.
I don't fit in. You feel the same, Mark, well, used to. I loved

the way you were with them. Them carryin on with their bad attitude, you used to slap them down, they were havin a laugh. Wass the army done to you? (*Takes off his shirt, shows his tattoo.*) Look.

Mark   Barry . . .

Barry   Thass British, thass us! Don't laugh at me, it's us. Show me yours.

Mark   Get off.

Barry   You were gonna wear it wid pride, you said. You didn't care who sees your red, white and blue, or who laughs, cos you ain't ending up like some black cunt. We are British, we are here! We kick arse with the best of them. God save the Queen, you told me that.

Mark   They don't want us here, Barry.

Barry   We were born here.

Mark   They don't care.

Lights up on the bar.

Glen *comes down. The screen turns blue again. Lads groan.*

Becks   Oh shut up, yer gettin on my tits now, the lot of yer.

Gina   How's my little prince then?

Glen   Awright.

Gina   Yer still gorgeous. (*Kisses him on the cheek.*)

Glen (*embarrassed*)   Mum?

Jimmy   You stopped cryin then?

Gina   Dad?

She holds up a beer glass to remind her father of her earlier threat.

I thought you were going to watch telly?

Glen   Nuttin's on.

Gina   Watch a video then. (*Gets a fiver from the till.*) Here, go down the video shop.

Glen   I don't want to go out.

Gina   You can't stay in here for ever, sweetheart. Sooner or later you're going to have to face those boys 'gain.

Glen   I know I have to face them again, Mum, but I don't want to do it now.

Gina   Calm down, I'm on your side, darlin. Go on, sit with the lads, watch the game. Go on, they don't bite.

Glen *joins* **Lee** *and the others. They all greet him warmly.*

Jason   Awright, Glen?

Phil   How you doing, son?

Lawrie   You want a Coke, Glen?

Glen   Yeah.

Gina   Yeah wat?

Glen   Yeah please.

Gina   Cheers, Lawrie.

Lawrie   Top this up as well, Gina.

Jason   Come on, Glen, cheer up.

Becks   Wat goes around, comes around, those black kids will get theirs.

Phil   This whole area is going down.

Becks   See, Glen, wat you have to do, is get a little gang of yer own, you and a few white lads.

Jason   Don't let Gina hear yer.

Lee   Or me!

Becks   There's nuttin wrong wid that?

Lee   You sure?

Becks   I've seen black gangs, Asian gangs, how can it be racist, if them boys are doing it? Get yerself some white boys, Glen, stick together, show sum pride. (*To screen.*) Unlike these wankers!

Lee (*to* **Glen**)   Oi, you ignore every word he said, you hear me?

Phil   Glen, come here, got a joke for yer. There's this black geezer right, Winston, nice fella, well thick. Anyway he's feelin a sick one morning, so he rings up his boss at work sayin (*puts on worst West Indian accent*), Ey, boss, I not come work today, I really sick. I got headache, stomach ache, and my legs hurt, I not come work. The boss goes, Oh Winston, you know I really need you today. It's important. Now, when I feel like this, I go to my wife, and tell her to give me sex. That makes me feel better and I can go to work. You should try that. Two hours later, Winston calls back, saying, Boss, boss, I did wat you said and I feel great, man! I be back at work real soon, boss. By the way, you got a nice house!

The boys roar with laughter.

Oops, I can see a smile, a smile is coming, he's smiling, he's smiling!

Boys cheer.

Lee   Is anyone watchin the match here?

Phil   What match?

Jason   Useless cunts.

Phil   Ere, Glen, come here. Yer mum still got that same boyfriend?

Glen   No. Why?

Phil   Nuttin.

Barry *and* **Mark** *come back.*

Becks   Barry my man, were you bin?

Jason   Have a nice tug, did yer? (*Rubs* **Barry**'s *head.*)

Barry   Don't.

Jason   Oooh, handbag.

Gina   We happy over there?

Mark   Sweet as, Gina.

Alan   Fancy a game, son?

Mark   I'm outta here.

Alan   Come on, one game.

Mark   Play me like you did my brother?

Alan   I have no idea what you mean.

Mark   Don't even bother.

Alan   All right then, I won't. But I bet you've fantasised about having a debate with someone like me. You want to shoot me down, find flaws in my twisted logic.

Mark   I've fantasised about kicking the shit out of someone like you.

Alan   That would be too easy. You and I agree on similar things.

Mark   Move.

Alan (*quotes*)   'They don't want us here, Barry.' I was in one of the cubicles. I overheard.

Mark   We got nuttin in common.

Alan   Let's see. (*Offers a cue-stick.*) Do you know what the main thing is that I hear people moan about? It's that, they don't think they can talk about it. They can't voice their concerns, how they feel, they're too scared to be called racists by the PC brigade. Now, I don't know about you, Mark, but I think we've got to get through that, because if people can't talk to each other, different communities, being honest, we are not going to get anywhere. So, come on. You and me, let's pave the way. If you want to stop people from being like me, then you had better start listening to people like me.

Mark *takes the cue-stick.*

Alan   So, army boy . . .

Mark   Ex.

Alan   What happened?

Mark   My CO was a racist wanker, so I smacked him one.

Alan   Nasty.

Mark   For him.

Alan   Do you know what you are going to do now?

Mark   You gonna give me a job? Let's get on with it.

Alan   Putting me straight. I like that. Do you watch TV, Mark?

Mark (*sarcastic*)   Once or twice.

Alan   All of those chat shows they have in the morning. *Trisha*, *Kilroy*, Richard & Judy.

Mark   Is there a point coming?

Alan   Any time they have some big issue to bang on about, they invite the general public, the great working class to have their say. Live debates, phone-ins, big mistake. I shudder when I hear them speak. Cringe. They are so inarticulate, they cannot string two sentences together. They are on live TV, and I'm screaming at the telly, articulate, you stupid sap. And their arguments, their points of view, Jesus Christ! So ignorant, stupid, dumb, deeply flawed, simplistic. It's obvious they have never read a book in their lives. I've seen black people on those programmes as well, son, and no offence, but it seems as though they've been eating retard sandwiches. Have you ever felt that way about them?

Mark No.

Alan Come on, Mark, honesty. Play the game.

Mark Yes.

Alan You hate the way they talk.

Mark Yes.

Alan You want to scream at them, they're letting the side down.

Mark Yes.

Alan Make your point, and make it well.

Mark You gonna make yours?

Alan Like me, you want to be better than that, but, unlike me, you know, wisely I might add, that can never happen. Not here.

Mark Wat?

Alan Look at us, Mark. (*Points at everyone.*) The white working class. You think it was an accident we are all as thick as shit? It's because of the powers that be. I know their game. Britain needs people like Lawrie to do the shit jobs. It can't have everyone bein a doctor or a lawyer, the economy would fall apart. Give them the shit life, shit education, the works. And do you know who we are going to blame for not getting ahead? You. Why? Because you're different, because it's convenient, because it's easier to blame you than it is to think about what's really going on, and the reason why we don't think is because we can't, and the reason we can't is the Hoo-ra-Henrys made sure of it. Spin us a tale, put it in the tabloids, we'll buy it. We'll blame anyone thass different for our own shortcomings. They want us to fight, they want us to fight you. We'll fight, but not the way they think. This is our country, we made it, and we don't belong in the gutter, because they say we do.

Mark But we do, yeah?

Alan   You're not dragging us down.

Mark   Gimme one good reason why I shouldn't wrap this
cue-stick round yer head.

Alan   Because I can help you.

Mark   By sending me back to ware I come from?

Alan   Eventually.

Mark   Convincing all my brothers and sisters to do the
same, work for you?

Alan   It's not as uncommon as you think. Some of our
European friends have had black and Jewish branches.
We're thinking of setting up our own ethnic liaison
committee.

Mark   Yer certifiable.

Alan   Don't tell me you're happy wid the way yer lot carry
on, especially round here. They can't fall out of bed without
getting into trouble.

Mark   I know how I feel, and yeah they make me sick to
be black. All they're doin is provin you and me right. But I
don't want to be right, any more, I want to be proved
wrong. I'm sick of being angry.

Alan   That's soppy talk.

Mark   I want to be who I want.

Alan   You are telling me you want to spend the rest of
your life walking round like an arsehole with your cap in
hand, waiting for the great white man to save you? He
wants to kill you. Have some respect for yourself, stand up
on your own two feet, make your own mark in the world, no
one else will do it for you.

Mark (*laughs*)   You sound like my old man.

Alan   Wise man, was he?

Mark   He thought he was.

Alan   What did he do?

Mark   Bus conductor.

Alan   How long?

Mark   Thirty-odd years.

Alan   And I bet he had to scrimp and save all his life.

Mark   Who doesn't?

Alan   But that is not what he wanted when he came here, I bet. Or are you telling me he left the sun and sea of the West Indies for the grey skies of London to be a bus conductor? The poor sod probably wanted to party all night, sleep with as many white women as possible, and smoke loads of shit.

Mark *bursts out laughing.*

Alan   You looked at him, and you thought, no way am I ending up like that. But you are, it's still happening. That is why you should go. Tell this country what to go and do with itself. No one is going to help you.

Mark   I don't want help.

Alan   You all want it, you're lost without us.

Mark   I want a chance.

Alan   But it us white people that's pulling all the strings, Mark. We'll decide how many chances you get. We're never going to change, so stop wishing. Show me one white person who has ever treated you as an equal, and I will show you a liar. The minute one of them says they are going to treat you as an equal, they're not. Because, in order to do that, they have to see you differently. It will never come as naturally as when they see another white person. All this multiculturalism. Eating a mango once a year at the Notting Hill Carnival is still a long way from letting your kids go to a school that is overrun with Pakis and blacks.

Mark   Wat is it wid you?

Alan   We come from different parts of the world, son, we have different ways of living.

Mark   I'm English.

Alan   No you're not.

Mark   I served in Northern Ireland. I swore an oath of allegiance to the flag.

Alan   Oh please.

Mark   How English are you? Where do you draw the line as to who's English. I was born in this country. And my brother. You're white, your culture comes from northern Europe, Scandinavia, Denmark. Your people moved from there thousands of years ago, long before the Celtic people and the Beeker people, what? You think cos I'm black, I don't read books. Where do you draw the line?

Alan   That's exactly the kind of ridiculous question we have to deal with.

Mark   Answer me.

Alan   The fact is, Mark, that the white British are a majority racial group in this country, therefore it belongs to the white British. If that was the case, what you're asking, we'd all be putting ourselves back into the sea. Because that is where we all originally came from, isn't it?

Mark   Yer full of shit.

Alan   We say that the people of European, white European descent are entitled to settle in Britain. Or the rest of Europe, where they are. We regard our racial cousins, the Americans, Canadians, as British. They've been implanted there over the centuries, now why should we take a time on it? The fact is the majority of blacks haven't been in this country for centuries, a few yes, maybe, but that's it. You've been here, predominantly, in your own numbers, three generations at most. That gives you squatters' rights. We're taking those squatters' rights away from you. You have given nothing to Britain, and you have never served any purpose in British history.

Mark   Oh, so the fact that thousands of black soldiers died during the war is lost on you.

Alan   Not as many as the Brits.

Mark   Or the fact that in the eighteenth century, there was a thriving black community, living right here?

Alan   Not as many as the Brits.

Mark   With their own pubs, churches, meeting places. Or the fact that in 1596, there were so many black slaves over here, working for their white owners, putting money in their pockets, doing all the work, that Queen Elizabeth saw them as a threat and wanted them out.

Alan   What are you on?

Mark   How many black Roman soldiers were here, when they came over and built your roads?

Alan   You're losing it.

Mark   Were you bullied at school, Alan? Couple of black kids nicked your dinner money? Or did your wife run off with a big black man? And I mean big black man? Or was it your mum?

Alan   If you're so smart, son, how come you still haven't caught up with us?

Mark   Cos you love pushing us down.

Alan   Well, push us back. You've had thousands of years. What are you waiting for, you useless bastards. Always some excuse. Can't you people take account for what you are doing to yourselves, instead of blaming us every five seconds?

Mark   You are to blame.

Alan   If you cannot hold your own to account for what they are doing, then we will be left to take drastic measures.

Mark   Is that right?

Alan   Lack of accountability creates anger, Mark, look at all the hate in the world, and it will twist some people's logic, just like Lawrie's, and flavour thought. Bad things are motivated purely by anger. You lot need to feel we will be held to account for what we've done, well, we need to feel it from you first.

Mark   You don't have the right.

Alan   Why's that?

Mark   Because yer white.

Alan   Who's the bigot now?

Mark   Go fuck yourself.

Alan   Face it, son, you're nothing but a ticked box. You will never be equal to us, and you know it.

Mark   You won't win. Thass wat I know.

Alan   We already have.

Mark (*chants*)   We shall not, we shall not be moved!

Alan   Mark?

Mark   We shall not, we shall not be moved, we shall not, we shall not be moved, we shall not, we shall not be moved, we shall not, we shall not be moved, we shall not, we shall not be moved, we shall not, we shall not be moved, we shall not, we shall not be moved, Baz!

Barry (*joins in*)   We shall not, we shall not be moved! We shall not, we shall not be moved –

Mark/Barry   We shall not, we shall not be moved! We shall not, we shall not be moved, And we'll go on, to win the great world cup, we shall not be moved!

Phil   You two pissed?

Barry/Mark   ENGLAND! (*Clap.*) ENGLAND! (*Clap.*)
ENGLAND! (*Clap.*) ENGLAND! (*Clap.*) ENGLAND!

Lawrie (*approaching*)   You awright, Alan?

Alan   They can't even see when someone is doing them a
favour. I've got a good mind to set you on him.

Lawrie   Why don't yer?

Alan   Don't be stupid.

Lawrie   I'll be careful.

Lee *comes out of the Gents.*

Lawrie   No fall-back on you. Say the word and he's dead.

Lee   Who's dead?

Alan   We are.

Lee   Who's dead, Lawrie?

Lawrie   No one.

Lee (*to* **Alan**)   You, fuck off.

Alan   Excuse me?

Lee   I'm talking to my brother.

Alan (*approaching*)   Another Scotch, Gina.

Lawrie   Take a shot.

Lee *throws the cue-stick across the table.*

Lawrie   Oh thass clever, Jimmy will love you if you break
his cue.

Lee   You touch Mark, I'll have yer.

Lawrie   Easy, tiger.

Lee   I've had enuff of yer shit, Lawrie.

Lawrie   Oh why are you still sticking up for them?

Lee   It weren't Mark that stabbed me.

Lawrie   They're scum.

Lee   I won't let you.

Lawrie   Who looked after yer, held yer hand every night while you had yer nightmares, Lee? Do you still see him when you shut yer eyes? That coon coming at yer with his knife?

Lee   It's me he tried to kill.

Lawrie   And I want to kill every one of them.

Lee   Yer never happy unless yer gettin stuck in on someone's head.

Lawrie   Go on, fuck off. Go back to yer posh bird.

Lee   If you weren't such a prick, you'd come live with us.

Lawrie   I ain't no ponce.

Lee   You need looking after.

Lawrie   Yer my kid brother, you don't look after me. God, I feel like I want to explode sometimes.

Lee   See.

Lawrie   I woulda killed someone by now if it weren't for Alan. I really would. I can feel myself wantin to do it sometimes. Every morning when I wake up. I wanna make a bomb or summin, go down Brixton and blow every one of them up.

Lee (*slaps his face*)   I'll kill you first. Do you want me to choose, Lawrie?

Lawrie   Do wat you want.

Lee   I want me brother.

Lawrie   I'm here.

Lee   Ask Alan about Reading, watch his face drop.

Lawrie Wat about it?

Lee Him and his lot were recruiting teenagers. One of them got a little excited, beat up some Asian kid. Alan, blindin geezer, didn't even wait for the Old Bill to breathe down his neck. He gave up that boy's name so fast, well desperate to save his arse. My new DS comes from Reading. He worked on the case. You want that to be you?

Lawrie That kid was stupid, he got caught.

Lee Why won't you ever listen to me?

Lawrie I ain't you, Lee.

Lee Fucking Dad.

Lawrie (*snaps*) Leave it!

Lee Don't think I won't warn him.

Lawrie You think thass gonna stop me?

The final whistle blows. The game is finished.

Jason Wat a load of fuckin bollocks.

Screen shows Kevin Keegan walking away with his head down. Sound of the crowd booing.

Yeah, nice one, lads, boo the cunt!

The boys join in the jeering.

Jimmy Southgate in midfield!

Phil Cole up front wid Owen!

Becks Lass game at Wembley!

Phil You see that? Hamman's wearing an England sweater.

Barry Who swapped jerseys?

Phil It's a number 4 he's wearin.

Becks Southgate.

Barry   Fuckin Kraut lover. We lose 1–0 and he's given him his jersey.

Becks's *phone rings.*

Becks (*answers*)   Awright, Rob? Yeah I know, fuckin disgrace ennit? Wat? Rob goes the fans are booing Keegan.

Jason   They wanna fuckin lynch him.

Mark   Come on, who's drinkin?

Phil   Yeah, go on then, with any luck, I might drown the memory of this day away.

Barry   Lass game at Wembley.

Mark   They're buildin a new one.

Barry   Won't be the same.

Becks   Awright, see yer in a bit. (*Hangs up.*) Rob's gonna come over. Well, come on, let's have some beer.

Jason   Yeah whose round is it, Becks?

Mark   Na yer awright, I'll get 'em in.

Becks   Cheers, Mark.

Mark   Barry?

Barry *goes with his brother.*

Jason   You are so bleeding tight, Becks. You ain't put yer hand in yer pocket all day, have yer?

Becks   Is it my fault our coloured friends over there are so generous? Come on, smile, yer cunts. We can still get to the finals, it's not impossible. We'll beat the Germans next year.

Phil   Oh yeah, we're really gonna hammer them on their own turf, ain't we?

Jason   Wat do you reckon the score will be, Becks, 5–1 to us?

Becks   Sod yer then.

Lee *approaches* **Barry** *and* **Mark**.

Lee   You gotta get out of here. Both of yer.

Mark   Why's that?

Lee   Lawrie's on the warpath, I don't know if I can hold him back.

Mark   You've never tried.

Lee   Come on, not now.

Barry   He's gonna have a pop in front of everyone?

Lee   He doesn't care. Look, juss go, awright.

Barry   Mark?

Mark   We're stayin.

Lee   He's gonna do some damage.

Mark   It's nice to know you care.

Lee   Yer my best mate.

Mark   Were.

Lee   Are!

Mark   Then why'd you say it, Lee?

Lee   I'm sorry, fer fuck's sake.

Mark   If that walrus wants to have a pop, let 'im.

A brick comes smashing through one of the windows.

Phil   Oh fuck!

Jason   Jesus!

Gina   Dad!

Phil   I'm cut.

Jimmy (*sees the window*)   Christ.

Phil   Bastards!

Gina You awright, Phil?

Phil Do I look it?

Gina Glen, get me the first-aid box.

Alan (*peers out of the window*) You had better get the police as well. There is a whole army of black kids out there.

Jason (*looks out*) Jesus!

Another brick comes flying through.

Oi! You black cunt.

Lee Shut up, Jase.

Jason They're lobbing bricks at us, wat you expect me to say?

Lee I'm going out there.

Lawrie (*concerned*) Lee?

Lee You stay.

Alan Lawrence. (*To* **Lee**.) He'll be all right.

Mark Lee, hold up, mate.

Lee Jimmy, call the police.

Gina Tell them if they step one foot in my pub, they'll be murders.

Mark *and* **Lee** *go out.* **Gina** *treats* **Phil***'s wounds with the first-aid box.*

Becks (*looks through the window*) Thass the little sod who took Glen's phone.

Glen *runs behind the bar and goes upstairs.*

Gina Glen, come back here, Glen!

Phil He'll be awright. He's a good kid.

Gina Oi, stop lookin at my tits.

Phil I can't help it. They're lovely.

Gina Excuse me?

Phil Yer lovely.

Gina Am I now?

Phil Yeah.

Gina You don't half pick yer moments, Philip.

Jimmy *approaches holding* **Glen** *by his ear.*

Jimmy He was only trying to sneak out through the back door.

Gina Wat you playing at?

Glen It's my problem right, I'm gonna deal wid dem.

Jimmy Listen to him.

Glen Wat you moanin for?

Jimmy There's a whole bleedin tribe out there, you wanna take them on? I've got a good mind to throw you out there myself.

Gina You wanna do summin? Go change the loo rolls in the Gents.

Glen *goes to do as he is told.*

Gina You call the police?

Jimmy They're comin.

Becks Might not need 'em now. Lee is doing the business, tellin them to back off.

Phil Send one of dem bastards in here, I'll do the business on them.

Lawrie Is Lee awright?

Becks He's doing the business. (*To* **Barry**.) And yer Mark. They make a good team.

Gina (*shouts by door*)   Mark? Lee? You find the bastards who broke my winder and tell them they owe me money.

Some of the crowd shout obscenities at **Gina**.

Yeah, fuck you an 'all. (*Shuts the door.*)

Mark *and* **Lee** *come back in.*

Barry   You awright, bruv?

Mark   Yeah. Thanks ever so much for helpin out there, Gina, very useful.

Gina   I weren't jokin, Mark, I want money for my winders.

Mark   It coulda bin worse.

Lee   They were well pissed.

Mark   Speakin of which. (*Goes to the loo.*)

Lee   I don't know how long me and Mark held them off for, they could come back. You call the police?

Jimmy   On way.

Gina   You sure that will do any good?

Lee   I dunno.

He catches sight of **Lawrie** *who looks like he's heading for the Gents.*

Lawrie? Lawrie!

Lawrie *in fact detours slightly and goes to the cigarette machine. Where he buys a packet of fags.*

Lawrie (*as calm as you like*)   Wat? (*Walks back to the pool table.*)

On the screen, Keegan is being interviewed.

Jimmy   Wass he goin on about, Jase?

Jason   He's only fuckin quit.

Phil   Wat?

Jason   Straight up, Keegan's quit!

Phil   Muppet.

Jimmy   Jesus.

Becks   Gotta tell Rob. (*Dials.*) Rob! Yeah, I know, shit game. Listen, Keegan's quit. He bloody has, it's juss come on. Yer bloody booin musta got to him. (*Aside.*) They don't know.

Jason   Course they don't know, they won't know till they leave the stadium.

Becks (*to phone*)   Well, I won't miss him, dozy sod. Yeah we'll see yer in a bit. (*Hangs up.*) Wass Keegan sayin, wass he moanin about?

Alan   He's going on about how he can't do it no more.

Becks   Bloody girl.

Lawrie   Wat? He said wat?

Becks   Summin about him wantin to spend time wid his family.

Lawrie *throws his drink. It almost hits the screen.*

Gina   Lawrie! Thass our screen.

Jimmy   Yer lucky you didn't hit it. Oi, I'm talkin to you, Lawrie? If yer old man was still alive, he'd tan yer arse.

Lawrie   Keegan's got no backbone, Jimmy, this whole country's lost its spine.

Jimmy   Oh piss off

Lawrie   We ruled the world.

Lee (*approaching*)   Broth.

Lawrie   Go play wid yer monkey friends.

Becks   Ease up, Lawrie.

Lawrie   Did I ask yer for anything?

Becks (*scared*)   Nuh, mate, you didn't.

Lawrie *catches* **Barry**'s *eye*.

Lawrie   You wanna have a pop? Well, come on then, black boy, show us how English you are.

Lee   Back off, Barry.

Barry   He challenged me.

Lee   He'll kill yer.

Lawrie   I'll have you, then those monkeys out there.

Gina *gets her baseball bat from behind the bar and waves it around.*

Becks   Whoa!

Gina   Not in my pub, you understand? Be told.

Jason   Yeah, Gina, watever you say.

Phil   I'm told.

Alan   Lawrie? (*Motions him to come over.*) Here!

Lee   Don't.

Gina   Leave him alone, Lee. He's a big boy.

Lawrie (*approaching*)   Why didn't you say anything?

Alan   Why won't you listen?

Lawrie   Cos I can't. Awright!

Alan   You won't even give yourself a chance. The smart-arses want to write you off as a brainless wanker, and you're letting them.

Lawrie   Juss let me have 'em. I won't mess up, I ain't stupid like that kid in Reading.

Alan   What do you know about Reading?

Lawrie   Got it from Lee. If this kid got himself caught, then thass his lookout.

Alan   The kid's name was Brian.

Lawrie   You gonna let me?

Alan   You remind me of him. Short fuse, kept running off on his own.

Lawrie   Come on, Alan.

Alan   He wouldn't listen. And I don't have time for people who refuse to listen, Lawrence!

Lawrie   Well, I'm tired of waiting. I wanted him. He wanted me. They all want it. Ask any coon. Let's juss stop all this fuckin about, and get it on. Lass one standing at the final whistle, wins England.

Alan   You gotta trust me, my way is the way forward.

Lawrie   No wonder this Brian kid got pissed off with yer. I mean fer fuck's sake, Alan, d'yer really think those smart-arses are gonna let us be as clever as them? I don't even want it.

Glen *is changing the loo paper in the Gents.* **Mark** *comes out of the next cubicle.*

Mark   You awright?

Glen *is getting frustrated as he cannot seem to get the finished loo roll off.*

Mark   Let me help.

Glen   No.

Mark   Don't be silly, there's nuttin to it.

Glen   Move.

Glen *shoves him, and as he does, a long kitchen knife drops from inside his jacket, on to the floor. He picks it quickly, but* **Mark** *has already seen it.*

Mark   Wat you doin wid that? Do you want me to go out and get yer mum, wat you doin wid that?

Glen   They fuck wid me, I'm gonna fuck wid them.

Mark   No, no that ain't the way, Glen.

Glen   You lot, you think yer so fuckin bad, I'll show you who's bad.

Mark   But this ain't the way. Duane and Tyrone yeah, they're juss boys. Not black boys, but juss boys. Stupid boys.

Glen   They're on us every day at school, all the white kids. Cos they think they're bad.

Mark   They're stupid boys, Glen.

Glen   You gonna move?

Mark   We are not all the same.

Glen   Move.

Mark   Juss gimme the knife.

Mark *moves to disarm him,* **Glen** *dodges* **Mark***, and stabs him repeatedly in the stomach.* **Mark** *drop to the floor.* **Glen** *cannot quite take in what he has done. He dashes out. Goes upstairs.*

Gina   You finished? Glen? Fine, ignore me why don't yer.

Lawrie *pops to the loo. He sees* **Mark***'s bleeding body and comes rushing out.*

Lawrie   We gotta go.

Alan   I don't waste time on losers, Lawrie, piss off.

Lawrie   Alan! We gotta go.

Alan   What have you done?

Lawrie   Nothing.

Jason (*comes running out of the loo*)   Oh shit!

Gina   Wat?

Jason   It's Mark.

Barry   Bruv? (*Sees* **Mark**.) Mark!

Lee   Don't touch him.

Barry   Get off me.

Lee   Let me see, let me see.

Barry   Ambulance!

Lee   Barry, listen . . .

Barry   Get off me.

Gina   Christ!

Lee   Get out.

Barry   Help him.

Lee   Barry, he's dead, look at me, he's dead.

Barry   Who fuckin did it!

Lee *spots* **Phil** *and* **Becks** *trying to leave.*

Lee   Ware you going? You can't leave.

Phil   Oh, come on, mate.

Lee   No one leaves! Who was last in here?

Lawrie (*feels* **Alan**'s *stare*)   Wat?

Lee   Lawrie?

Lawrie   Oh yeah, here we go.

Lee   You were lass in the toilets.

Lawrie   It weren't me.

Alan   You bloody fool.

Lawrie   Alan, it weren't me, I saw him thass all.

Barry *runs at* **Lawrie**, *who holds him down, hitting him twice in the face.* **Lee** *pulls him off.*

Lee   Lawrie, enough, get off him.

Lawrie   I'm gonna line you up next to him.

Lee   Where's the knife, wat you do with it?

Lawrie *spits in his brother's face.*

Lee   Lawrence Bishop. I am arrresting you on suspicion of murder, you do not have to say anything, but it may harm yer defence if you do not mention when questioned something you may rely on in court. (**Lawrie** *spits in his face again.*) Anything you do say will be given in evidence. You made me choose.

Jason   This is fucked up.

Becks   Let us go, Lee.

Lee   No.

Jimmy *comes out, dragging **Glen** behind him.*

Gina   Dad?

Jimmy   Gina.

Gina   Wat? Wat!

Jimmy *throws the bloodstained knife on to the bar.*

Gina   No!

Becks   Oh shit.

Lee   Glen, come here.

Gina   No, Glen!

Lee   I said come here.

Barry   It was you!

Lee   Barry, juss back off, yeah.

Barry   Don't you fuckin touch me!

Glen   He's a black bastard, they all are.

Gina   Shut up.

Jimmy   Jesus.

Gina   Hard enuff for yu now, Dad?

Jimmy   Gina?

Alan   Rivers of blood.

Barry   Yu shut yer mout, I'll kill yer. I'll kill all of yer. Come on, come on! Who wants me, come on! Yer fuckin white cunts, all of yer! All of yer. Cunts! Come on! Yer white cunts.

Lee   Barry?

Barry   No.

He wipes the paint off his face.

No! No. (**Lee** *approaches.*) Fuck off. Get away from me.

Lawrie   Monkey lover.

Jason (*peers through window*)   Oh shit, they're only coming back.

Phil   Who?

Jason   Fuckin blacks.

Lawrie   No point playin games, Alan.

Alan   I don't know you.

Lawrie   No matter what, it'll come to this.

Sound of police sirens approaching.

Lee   Barry?

Barry   No.

Lee (*to* **Barry**)   Don't lose yerself.